AMERICA

IN THE NEW WORLD ORDER

THOMAS J. HUGHES

FOREWORD BY DON STEWART

Website: http://www.hopeforourtimes.com
Facebook: www.facebook.com/TomHughesEndTimes
Twitter: @PastorTomHughes
Instagram: pastortomhughes
Amazon author page: amazon.com/author/thomasjhughes

Third Printing
ISBN: 978-0-9976052-0-4

Printed in the United States of America

ACKNOWLEDGMENT

Thanks to Tom Gilbreath for his
help in keeping me on track, his vast
knowledge of the issues at hand,
and for fact-checking the material.

TABLE OF CONTENTS

FOREWORD

From a distance this book may appear to have been written to Christians. On the contrary, while it contains material that will be invaluable to professing Christians, it is written for stay-at-home moms, working parents, city employees, stock brokers, public officials, first responders, young adults, retirees.... You get the idea. *America in the New World Order* was written for anyone who watches the nightly news, reads a newspaper, or engages in conversation with family and friends.

This book will help readers connect the dots regarding the U.S. economy and the political landscape. It answers the questions we all ask. What is going to happen to America, and what does it mean for me and my family?

Tom Hughes is a gifted communicator with an uncanny ability to help the reader make sense out of the chaos that seems to be engulfing our country and the world. We need

AMERICA IN THE NEW WORLD ORDER

to understand how our nation fits into the fast approaching New World Order.

I strongly encourage you to make this the next book you read, then encourage others to do the same. You will be better off for it. Tom is one of the rising voices today and many have anticipated this book, including me.

-Don Stewart
Lecturer, Bible Scholar, Bible Prophecy Teacher, Author
educatingourworld.com

ONE

NEW WORLD ORDER

At the Biltmore Theater on April 28, 1968, something different happened on Broadway. The cast mingled with the audience as incense burned on stage. Slowly the lights went down. From the darkness a cosmic sound effect wrenched itself into music. As the lights came back up, the cast moved onto the stage in carefully choreographed slow motion.

At last, a lone female voice began to sing.

> *When the moon is in the Seventh House*
> *And Jupiter aligns with Mars*
> *Then peace will guide the planets*
> *And love will steer the stars.*

Hair became the first musical to start off-Broadway, then move to Broadway. The night of its debut on "The Great White Way," the counter-culture went mainstream. New York society celebrated draft avoidance, illicit drugs, casual sex... and the beginning of a new world order.

After the single voice declared that "love will steer the stars," a full-throated chorus sang:

> *This is the dawning of the age of Aquarius*
> *Age of Aquarius*
> *Aquarius!*
> *Aquarius!*[1]

It was more than a song. It was an anthem of change. With those words and with that music, a generation of young people declared that they were not their parents. Materialism, nationalism, and judgmentalism would be replaced by love, peace, and understanding—the Age of Aquarius.

Only it didn't happen.

The eighteen-year-olds of 1968 became the forty-year-olds of 1990, and the sixty-six-year-olds of 2016. Now, when they think of the parents they once disdained, they consider them members of "the greatest generation." They wish they had done as well.

Why did the age of Aquarius dawn and die in the same hour? In his wisdom, Solomon said, "That which has been is what will be, that which is done is what will be done, and there is nothing new under the sun" (Ecclesiastes 1:9).

---

1. *Hair*, lyrics by James Rado and Gerome Ragni. Music by Galt MacDermot. © Sony/ATV Music Publishing LLC, Universal Music Publishing Group.

At some point in every generation, someone stands up and says, "Let's be the first ones to really get it right. Let's do the obvious thing so that we can live long and happy lives together."

But "the obvious thing" isn't always the same thing to everyone. Few today think well of the Nazi version of "the obvious thing." The Nazis proposed a Third Reich, sometimes called a "Tausendjähriges Reich," meaning "Thousand Year Reign." Hitler spoke of his new world order lasting a thousand years because he wanted to create a millennial reign—like in the Bible, but different.

History is replete with new world orders—starting in Genesis.

LET US MAKE A NAME

After the flood, God told mankind through Noah, "Be fruitful and multiply, and fill the earth" (Genesis 9:1). They did well with parts one and two of that plan. They were fruitful. They multiplied. But they did not "fill the earth." They filled one small spot on the earth.

For the first few generations following the flood, they stayed in the mountains, apparently fearing another deluge. They should have trusted God instead of their fears. After the flood, He had made an immutable promise.

"I set My rainbow in the cloud, and it shall be for the sign of the covenant between Me and the earth…. The waters shall never again become a flood to destroy all flesh" (Genesis 9:13, 15).

The people feared a flood that God said would never happen. They didn't believe God's promise, so they didn't obey His command.

Finally, they migrated from the mountains of modern-day Turkey to the plains of modern-day Iraq. Though they moved down from the mountains, they kept together instead of following God's command and spreading out into the world. Their leaders, probably with Nimrod in charge, worked to make sure they stayed together. He knew that once the people had been on the plains for a while, no longer fearing a flood, they would drift in different directions.

Nimrod wanted to keep the people close enough to be centrally governed. More people in one place meant more power and more wealth for those in charge.

To keep the entire population of earth in a relatively small area and continue their one-world government, Nimrod and his friends came up with an audacious plan. "They said, 'Come, let us build ourselves a city, and a tower whose top is in the heavens; let us make a name for ourselves, lest

we be scattered abroad over the face of the whole earth'"
(Genesis 11:4).

Specifically to keep everyone together rather than filling
the earth, they began building a magnificent city whose
centerpiece was a tower rising high into the heavens.

Then God entered the scene;

> But the LORD came down to see the city and
> the tower which the sons of men had built.
> And the LORD said, 'Indeed the people are
> one and they all have one language, and this
> is what they begin to do; now nothing that
> they propose to do will be withheld from them.
> Come, let Us go down and there confuse their
> language, that they may not understand one
> another's speech.' So the LORD scattered
> them abroad from there over the face of all
> the earth, and they ceased building the city.
> Therefore its name is called Babel, because
> there the LORD confused the language of all
> the earth; and from there the LORD scattered
> them abroad over the face of all the earth"
> (Genesis 11:5-9).

They refused the command to "fill the earth," so "the
LORD scattered them abroad over the face of all the

earth." The planet would not have a one-world government again for many thousands of years.

ONE WORLD, ONE PEOPLE

Today the words "New World Order" are most often associated with a speech by President George H. W. Bush to a joint session of Congress on September 11, 1990. The Gulf War had begun a month earlier with Operation Desert Shield. The combat phase, Operation Desert Storm, would not begin until January.

President Bush was not the first to use the phrase "New World Order," but he said it in a way that sent conspiracy buffs running for cover.

At the time Bush spoke, the Soviet Union was only a year away from final collapse. The Berlin Wall had already come down, and Eastern Europe was moving out of the Soviet sphere of influence. From late 1989 through 1991, the "old world order" was disappearing. Bush knew that a new one would inevitably replace the old, and he wanted America to shape it.

Who can blame a president for wanting to lead the world out of its fallen past and into a new utopian future? The President's level of hope rivaled that of Woodrow Wilson who famously referred to World War I as "a war to end all wars."

"Out of these troubled times," Bush said, "our fifth objective—a new world order—can emerge: a new era.... An era in which the nations of the world, East and West, North and South, can prosper and live in harmony. A hundred generations have searched for this elusive path to peace, while a thousand wars raged across the span of human endeavor. Today that new world is struggling to be born, a world quite different from the one we've known. A world where the rule of law supplants the rule of the jungle. A world in which nations recognize the shared responsibility for freedom and justice."[2]

President Bush saw the world on the cusp of a harmony searched for by a hundred generations. After a thousand wars, and especially with the end of the cold war, he saw the United States and the United Nations leading humanity into an era of peace. Those were heady days for people who believe that the arc of history tends toward global government.

But things didn't turn out as planned.

THINGS FALL APART

We know for certain that the present world order cannot hold. Technological advances are allowing even poor

---

2. Bush, George H. W. Address before a Joint Session of US Congress, September 11, 1990.

countries to possess vast arsenals of sophisticated bombs with missiles to carry them. As nations grow more secular, individuals become more susceptible to spiritual corruption and radicalism.

Economically, every nation on the face of the earth stands on precarious ground. The world's central banks use all their tricks every day just to keep their economies afloat. Long term, it is untenable.

- The United States remains the world's only superpower, but internal forces of societal decay and moral corruption threaten that position.

- The European Union faces the same internal putrefaction. It remains economically powerful, but its borders are collapsing under the weight of a massive influx of people whose beliefs and culture are utterly unlike those of the European countries they are entering.

- Japan, South Korea, and the other Asian powers make money, but they never seem to find economic stability.

- North Korea cannot feed its citizens, but builds nuclear weapons, and threatens the world.

• China, another nuclear power, looms to the east. Its military ambitions seem to know no bounds. Though an industrial colossus, the communist regime at its heart continues to make its economy uncertain.

• Russia remains enigmatic. It holds the largest arsenal of nuclear warheads of any nation, along with ICBMs able to carry the nukes anywhere in the world. Its people are suffering, yet it makes forays into sovereign nations. So far, none of those nations belong to NATO or the EU, but that could change overnight. More and more, its attention seems to have turned south to the Middle East and its oil.

• Africa and the Middle East cannot build securely because bands of cutthroat terrorists keep roiling the peace.

• Then there is Israel. Though geographically only about the size of Vermont, Israel remains the center of world attention and consternation.

As William Butler Yeats wrote, "Things fall apart; the centre cannot hold."[3]

---

3. From "The Second Coming" by William Butler Yeats, 1919

OUR FOCUS

The Bible teaches about two New World Orders coming at or near the end of the age. Both will be identified with single world leaders. The first is the Antichrist. His kingdom will be big, but it won't last long. After that will come a world order that never ends. It, too, will be identified with its Leader—the Lord Jesus Christ.

In this book, we will look at the stage now being set for the Antichrist's rule, but always in the light of the eternal Kingdom to follow.

TWO

BEASTS AND KINGS

In Revelation 13, God gave John a vision of the Antichrist's New World Order taking shape.

> "I stood on the sand of the sea. And I saw a beast rising up out of the sea, having seven heads and ten horns, and on his horns ten crowns, and on his heads a blasphemous name. Now the beast which I saw was like a leopard, his feet were like the feet of a bear, and his mouth like the mouth of a lion. The dragon gave him his power, his throne, and great authority. And I saw one of his heads as if it had been mortally wounded, and his deadly wound was healed. And all the world marveled and followed the beast. So they worshiped the dragon who gave authority to the beast; and they worshiped the beast, saying, 'Who is like the beast? Who is able to make war with him?' And he was given a mouth speaking great things and blasphemies, and he was given

authority to continue for forty-two months"
(Revelation 13:1-5).

Verse 2 says, "The dragon gave him his power, his throne,
and great authority." Revelation 12:9 and 20:2 identify
the dragon as Satan himself. "The great dragon was cast
out, that serpent of old, called the Devil and Satan, who
deceives the whole world" (Revelation 12:9).

Verses 6 and 7 say the Antichrist "opened his mouth in
blasphemy against God, to blaspheme His name, His tabernacle, and those who dwell in heaven. It was granted to
him to make war with the saints and to overcome them."

The Antichrist will rail against God, against God's
name, against the rebuilt tabernacle, against those who
were raptured out of the world, and against those who
will have come to faith in Christ during the tribulation.

> "Authority was given him over every tribe,
> tongue, and nation. All who dwell on the
> earth will worship him, whose names have
> not been written in the Book of Life of the
> Lamb slain from the foundation of the world"
> (Revelation 13:7-8).

"Authority…over every tribe, tongue, and nation" means
that the Antichrist will be given the leadership of a one-
world government. It will be a kind of global federalism

where the nations will maintain their traditional names, borders, and much of their old authority to make and enforce laws. But a new worldwide government will exist above them. The worldwide government will have the authority to tax and police, as well as create and enforce laws and regulations. Its power will supersede the power of the nations.

WORKING FOR A NEW WORLD ORDER

When the Antichrist comes on the scene, a one-world government will have already been formed. The ten kings of Revelation 17:12-13 will already be in power. Later, they will step aside in favor of the beast who will run the one-world government with ruthless efficiency. At least in the beginning, it will seem efficient.

The world is full of organizations presently working toward a New World Order and a one-world government. They are well-connected and filled with ultra-rich people who see global governance as the only viable future for mankind. This is not about conspiracy theories, but real groups that we know exist, and about whose agendas we know a great deal.

Yes, there are wild theories out there. Television dramas have taught an entire generation that the obvious answer is never the correct one—that we should look for a dark cabal lurking behind the scenes, pulling the strings behind all big events.

In the 1997 film, *Conspiracy Theory*, the character played by Mel Gibson is an over-the-top, out in left field conspiracy nut. At one point he admits, "A good conspiracy is unprovable."

An entire subculture of people exists who spend their time trying to prove "unprovable conspiracies." It may be fun to read, and sometimes they make interesting points, but we're not going there. We're talking here about groups that, while secretive, make their positions known in a variety of ways. Many of their members are also well known.

It's no theory that behind-the-scenes power brokers have vast influence on world events. A few decades ago, American politics were dominated by what everyone called "smoke-filled rooms." Today they meet over lattès instead of cigars, but they still meet. There are circles of power, inner circles, and inmost circles. Is that a conspiracy theory? No, it's obvious. History books are full of wheels within wheels, plans within plans.

According to the Bible, the inmost circles will eventually coalesce their power around the ten kings of Revelation 17. These will be "kings," but without kingdoms. They will have enormous influence, wealth, and power, in every way like royalty, but they will not be heads of state.

"The ten horns which you saw are ten kings who have received no kingdom as yet, but they receive authority for one hour as kings with the beast. These are of one mind, and they will give their power and authority to the beast" (Revelation 17:12-13).

The ten "kings" will establish a one-world government, then cede their power to the one-world dictator. Like kingmakers throughout history, they will probably believe they can control their man. They will expect to be the power behind the throne—not realizing that they are mere pawns, and that the power behind this throne will be Satan himself.

DEMOCRACY'S DECLINE

To gain the kind of power described in the Bible, the Antichrist must diminish (without appearing to) "government of the people, by the people, for the people."

Conventional wisdom says history is moving toward representative government. Over the last two hundred years, democracy has spread to most of the world—in name, if not always in practice. The world's great experiment with republican forms of government, however, is not doing well.

Please understand that I think it's the best form of human government yet devised. Until Christ returns to rule and reign, I want to live in a republic. I want a meaningful vote and representative rule.

But a republic must possess a certain level of moral fitness in order to operate well. That fitness shows itself in small things like civility and in large things like placing country before party or self. In America, the divide between Republican and Democrat has not been this wide since the Civil War. Even within each political party, antagonisms are at an all time high. We no longer simply question an opponent's policy choices, but his character, and sometimes that of his children. Lobbyists have become so good at their jobs that they can derail legislation even when all sides agree on it.

Democracies across the world face similar struggles. They seem incapable of solving even minor problems. Extremists and special interests exacerbate divisions. As governments grow more intrusive, they become correspondingly less efficient.

This hits close to home. U.S. military veterans have died in significant numbers because the government-run health care they were promised is a mess. When government identifies a problem, it pumps in vast sums of money to fix it...inevitably making the original problem worse, and creating new ones along the way.

The Antichrist will come with a simple answer. He will make people believe he can build a government that works and create an economy with widespread prosperity. But to build his utopia, he will claim to need special powers. No one will say "dictator." They will say "benevolent, efficient, innovative, and effective."

On several occasions, President Obama has lamented the lack of power he has as a mere President. In 2013 he said, "The problem is that I'm the President of the United States, I'm not the emperor of the United States. My job is to execute laws that are passed."

He was lamenting the lack of efficiency of a government with checks and balances. Bypassing all that, giving vast governing authority to a single person eliminates gridlock. A dictator can efficiently create and execute laws. In a time of turmoil, the advantages of consolidating power in one man will fall like ripe fruit in the hand. A desperate world will believe that a single man of extraordinary skill and charisma can end the chaos, make the trains run on time, and help everyone make money and feel safe.

He will not come across as a tyrant, but as an extension of democracy. At first, his rule may be presented as a temporary solution to an impending crisis. In any case, the masses will be made to feel they chose all this for themselves. Behind-the-scenes power brokers long ago took over the mainstream media, and they will sell the Antichrist like soap.

You and I are currently watching the development of this New World Order. It's been in play for many, many years and now it's taking form before our eyes.

UTOPIA / DYSTOPIA

H. G. Wells died in 1946 at age seventy-nine. We chiefly remember him for writing *The Time Machine, The Invisible Man, The War of the Worlds*, and other early science fiction thrillers. He was a prolific writer, putting out hundreds of books during his lifetime.

He also inspired other writers, though not always in positive ways. Aldous Huxley said that *Brave New World* was an answer to Wells' utopian novels, *Men Like Gods* and *A Modern Utopia*. With *Brave New World*, Huxley showed that even a man as brilliant and inventive as H.G. Wells couldn't create a real utopia—not even in his imagination.

Wells not only believed in a one-world government, he believed in a fascist one-world government. Here are some features of his utopian view of the future.

• In 1936, he forecast the coming of a "World Brain." He envisioned something like the Internet combined with AI (artificial intelligence). Many scientists, including Stephen

Hawking, have warned that a real AI might take over everything, and either rule or destroy mankind. Interesting, but hardly utopian. In a recent *Time Magazine* editorial, longtime AI proponent and defender, Eric Schmidt, warned of the need for AI designers to "establish best practices to avoid undesirable outcomes.... There should be verification systems that evaluate whether an AI system is doing what it was built to do.... AI will reflect the values of those who build it." It makes you glad Hitler didn't have an AI with which to reflect and amplify his values.

- Wells believed that in the future, every person would have an identity number, and the World Brain would know all the basic facts about each individual.

- A special squad of "elites" would solve all problems. Like many in his day, Wells believed that smart, emotionally uninvolved, scientifically-minded people could solve anything if given the authority to do so. He believed that most problems have only one solution and that without emotional entanglements, the "elites" would quickly see it.

- The elites would have full access to the World Brain's population database, knowing the whereabouts and basic data on every person in the world at all times.

• People considered "plain," "dull," or "stupid" would either be exterminated or sent away to an abandoned island.

• He also believed that the "elites" would take on the job of "rewiring the human mind."

How's that for utopia? In his book, *The New World Order*, Wells wrote, "Countless people will hate the New World Order and will die protesting against it."[4]

Ya think?

TOTALITARIAN UNIVERSITY

George Orwell also wrote what is called a "dystopian" novel in response to the silly utopian ideas popular in those days. He called it *1984*. Orwell wrote, "During times of universal deceit, telling the truth becomes a revolutionary act."

For a taste of what he meant, talk to an outspoken evangelical college student in America today. Better yet, talk to a professor, even a liberal one, who likes to ask hard questions on both sides of issues. In academia today, just asking a thought-provoking question can get you in trouble. Think about that. Asking politically incorrect (i.e.

4. Wells, H.G. *New World Order*. Minneapolis: Filiquarian Publishing, 2007.

evangelical Christian or politically conservative) questions in an academic environment gets people fired.

Ten years ago, the president of Harvard noted that men hold most of the top university positions in science. This is well recognized in academic circles, and seen as evidence of gender bias in the ways boys and girls are raised. The Harvard president mentioned the possibility that it might have to do with "issues of intrinsic aptitude." He said, "There is reasonably strong evidence of taste differences between little girls and little boys that are not easy to attribute to socialization."

In other words, he stated the mere possibility that boys and girls are born different including, perhaps, a slight difference in either interest in or aptitude for science. He didn't say males have more "intrinsic aptitude" for science than females. He suggested it as a possibility worth looking into.

The academic community in America and around the world went apoplectic. Some women immediately walked out of the conference. Many left in tears. Criticism poured in from campuses everywhere. How dare he ask that question? How dare he suggest that anyone ask that question?

Yet, it is undeniable that more males (certainly not all, but more) reach the highest levels of math, science, and engineering. While everyone recognizes the same statistics, most feminists see those statistics as evidence of sexism. I'm not saying who's right, just that science ceases to be science when it must adhere to political correctness. No one should be banished for simply asking the question.

It was a foretaste of university life to come. In the decade that followed, free inquiry and free speech have been dying a horrible death. Scientists tend to either avoid controversy entirely, or design their research to back up the already accepted orthodoxy among their fellow academics.

If you can lose your job for asking politically incorrect questions, imagine what awaits those who actually tell the politically incorrect truth.

BIG LIES

The nature of the Antichrist's New World Order requires the rise of totalitarianism in places of influence like the campus. The Antichrist's rule will require followers who are willing to believe without question several incompatible ideas all at the same time. To that end, political correctness, as now practiced on American university campuses, may prove to be indispensable.

Political correctness serves as a tool for opinion makers. It changes as their needs change. Who would have thought in the early days of the feminist movement that liberal champions of that cause would one day also champion a religion whose holy book equates women's rights with those of goats? But here we are. Those who claim to be feminists tend also to be defenders of Islam.

The ability to shape public opinion, to guide people into passionate belief in illogical positions, seems like a parlor trick. It's uncanny. You see it but can't believe it. Hitler's Germany was full of people who passionately believed in the Nazi cause. Just a few years later, most of those same people were embarrassed and horrified to have ever believed such insanity.

The madness did not strike them all. Most of those who walked close to God and the Bible did not fall for the lie. The majority of scientists (at least those who were not Jews) tended to accept the fascist deception. Wealthy people, educated people, and smart people fell for the lie. But for the most part, even simple people who were Christian "true-believers"—the kind society fears—were not duped by Hitler's deceit.

As America collectively, and Americans individually, reject God, the nation becomes more vulnerable to the Big Lie. Those who openly reject God become ripe pickings for the cult of personality that will surround the Antichrist.

THREE

SUBORDINATION OF NATIONS

In June of 2015, Pope Francis issued his encyclical on climate change. It called for global entities to wrest control from local governments. "International negotiations," he wrote, "cannot make significant progress due to positions taken by countries which place their national interests above the global common good."[5]

In other words, nations tend to act in their own best interests, and he thinks that's a problem when it comes to climate change and other issues. So he called for "global regulatory norms...to impose obligations and prevent unacceptable actions."

Where do these new regulatory norms come from? Pope Francis explained, "There is urgent need of a true world political authority.... One authoritative source of

---

5. Pope Francis, Evangelium Vitae, Encyclical letter on On Care for Our Common Home, May 24, 2015, w2.vatican.va/.../papa-francesco_20150524_enciclica-laudato-si.html

oversight and coordination…which lays down rules for admissible conduct in the light of the common good."

But even "a true world political authority" might change its opinions if the masses are allowed to choose their leaders. So Pope Francis called on the world to enact climate change laws in a godlike manner, written on unalterable tablets of stone. He said, "Continuity is essential, because policies related to climate change and environmental protection cannot be altered with every change of government."

In democracies, changes of government come from the will of the people. He is therefore calling for the subjugation of the people's will to that of an elite few who write unalterable laws. As a man of faith, you would expect him to recognize that those kinds of laws can only be written by God.

Pope Francis called for a global governmental entity that can override nations acting in their own interest. He wants to create a world where climate policies cannot be changed as a result of free elections. That means he wants a global government that is responsive only to a few elites.

So again we see the pattern. Make the power global, and coalesce that power into the hands of a few.

GOVERNMENT BY TRADE AGREEMENT

One of the cleverest means of creating global government is to create trade agreements that establish their own governmental entities. In some cases, the new governments created by the trade agreements supersede the governments that created the trade agreements in the first place. Something as benign sounding as a trade deal can be the foot in the door for the Antichrist's New World Order.

The Trans-Pacific Partnership (TPP) makes a great example. Ostensibly, it's about free trade between the nations of Australia, Canada, Japan, Malaysia, Mexico, Peru, the United States, Vietnam, Chile, Brunei, Singapore, and New Zealand.

TPP creates a new governmental entity called the Trans-Pacific Partnership Commission, or just "the Commission." It isn't global. It only covers the nations that sign on to it, but the twelve now on board represent forty percent of the global economy. And more nations have been invited to join. U.S. Secretary of State John Kerry recently invited China and Russia to join TPP.

Even a cursory look at this agreement shows that it's not so much about trade as it is about coalescing power. Article 27 of the TPP says, "The Parties hereby establish a Trans-Pacific Partnership Commission....The Commission shall... consider any proposal to amend or modify this Agreement...(and) take such other action as the Parties may agree."

The Commission is in fact a government, and in certain areas that new government's authority exceeds that of the U.S. Congress. For instance, the Commission can change the rules of the TPP any way it wants and Congress can do nothing about it.

TPP LAWS AND COURTS

To enforce its will, the TPP provides for "Arbitration Tribunals." These have the authority to impose multi-billion dollar fines so large that even the United States Treasury would have to sit up and take notice. Any government that does not comply with the Commission's orders will pay dearly.

The TPP contains a clause stating that "each Party affirms its commitment to implement the multilateral environmental agreements to which it is a party." In other words, TPP signatories will be compelled to implement everything those countries have agreed to at Climate Conferences such as the 2030 Agenda. Even if Congress does not ratify such deals, TPP tribunals will have the power to sanction any nation that does not fully comply.

As a trade deal, TPP makes little sense. It not only gives foreign corporations full access to American markets; it gives them advantages over American companies.

It also removes nation of origin labeling. The government of Brunei bans Christians from celebrating Christmas except in secret. Maybe as a Christian, you would like to boycott Brunei products. Guess what? You can't. TPP makes it illegal to label where a product comes from. So no more "Made in the U.S.A."

As a private citizen, you might learn that a certain product comes from Brunei. If you decide to organize a boycott of that product, under TPP you can be sued.

Suppose one of the trading partners has an outbreak of mad cow disease in its cattle herds. During such an outbreak, wouldn't you want to know where the beef you are buying came from? Not allowed! They apparently inserted this provision to help countries known for subpar products have equal footing with those famous for their quality.

Nation of origin labeling at least has something to do with trade. TPP has all sorts of features that have nothing to do with trade. It has provisions on immigration, wealth redistribution, education, human rights, including children's rights (which puts its reach into every home), gay rights, same-sex marriage, gun control, healthcare, women's reproductive rights, abortion, and sustainable development.

The TPP Commission has the authority to protect, among other things, fish, seals, trees, and wetlands. That means it controls the water and the land. It has the authority to stop all kinds of land and water pollution. Sounds great until you realize that pollution is often simply a matter of opinion. The Commission has the right to tell people where they can and cannot live, and where they can and cannot work.

Obviously, these nations could have made a trade agreement without creating a supernational government. What's really going on? This is about ceding national sovereignty to international agencies. It's taking a giant step toward one-world government, the Antichrist, and Armageddon. It's about placing everyone under the control of a ruling elite that ordinary citizens cannot vote on, remove, or replace.

Massive change is coming, and coming fast. And it all fits perfectly with Bible prophecy.

2030 AGENDA

In September of 2015, the 193 member states of the United Nations General Assembly unanimously passed

"The 2030 Agenda for Sustainable Development." The UN describes the 2030 Agenda in utopian terms. "We are determined to take the bold and transformative steps which are urgently needed to shift the world onto a sustainable and resilient path. As we embark on this collective journey, we pledge that no one will be left behind."

"No one will be left behind" really means, "No one will be allowed to opt out."

Implementing the 2030 Agenda will cost around $5 trillion per year. So, over the course of the fifteen year agenda, we're talking about $75 trillion. We're so used to hearing gigantic numbers, that it may take a moment for that to sink in. The U.S. budget for fiscal year 2015 was $3.8 trillion. That includes entitlement programs, the military, everything!

In other words, the 193 nations of the UN General Assembly voted unanimously to create a governmental entity that is significantly larger than the government of the United States.

To better understand those numbers, think of this. The entire gross domestic product (GDP) for the United States in 2015 was less than $18 trillion. Investopedia defines GDP as, "The total dollar value of all goods and services produced over a specific time period." Annual GDP would be the value of all the goods and services produced by every person and business in the United States during that year. It's an almost unfathomable number. Yet the United Nations plans to spend four times that much implementing the 2030 Agenda over the next fifteen years.

Two questions immediately come to mind. Where are they going to get such massive sums of money, and what are they going to do with it? To answer the first question, simply take a look in the mirror…because they're counting on you to pay for it. If you're an American, they think you've been living at a level that is unsustainable, and they plan to cut your lifestyle down to size.

TAXING PROSPERITY INTO OBLIVION

UN officials don't use the "t" word—tax—but they dance all around it. To make the 2030 Agenda happen will require a level of taxation the UN does not yet have the authority to levy. But if the nations are in any way serious about the Agenda, they will create a method of taxation that goes to a whole new level. The power to tax is real power indeed.

Will they get that kind of money? Probably not. One of the private citizens pushing the Agenda has been Microsoft founder, Bill Gates. In 2015, he said, "There's certainly no chance that that amount of money will be available next year.... We'd be doing very well to have anywhere near that amount of money available by 2030."

But they're going to try, and in trying they can do tremendous harm without doing any good at all.

So what do they want to do with this previously unheard of amount of money? They seem to think they're going to create a modern utopia. The 2030 Agenda "Preamble" says, "We are resolved to free the human race from the tyranny of poverty."

That fits perfectly with item number one on the Agenda. "End poverty in all its forms everywhere." Fighting poverty is good, but their plans to eradicate it will destroy far more prosperity than it creates.

There is a reason Jesus said, "You have the poor with you always" (Mark 14:7). He did not mean we should refuse to help the poor. Plenty of scripture makes it clear that the poor have a special place in God's heart. But until Christ returns, we will have the poor with us. Poverty will end when He rules with "a rod of iron" (Revelation 12:5, 19:15). Jesus ruling with an iron scepter is a good thing. The UN with that kind of power, I find disturbing.

The United Nations cannot eradicate poverty, and they know it. The point is not to solve the problem. The point is to use the mandate of the nations to consolidate power for the few. If they truly intended to end poverty with a Robin Hood approach—steal from the rich and give to the poor—they would disrupt or destroy all the wealth-generating businesses and people on the face of the earth. They can't make everyone rich, but they might be able to make most people poor.

Item number ten promises to, "Reduce inequality within and among countries." This too is wealth redistribution, but on an unheard of scale. It puts the UN in the middle of everything. Reducing inequality "within" countries puts the UN inside every nation's business community, every town's school district, and every business in the world. Reducing inequality "among" nations puts the UN in charge of wealth redistribution among nations!

Remember that the authors of the 2030 Agenda do not believe that the American lifestyle is "sustainable." They're not trying to raise world prosperity to American levels. Except for protecting the ultra-rich, they want to lower Americans' living standards to fall more in line with a "sustainable" future. These people believe that for the benefit of "Mother Earth" they need to make America and Americans poor.

Sadly, some of our own leaders believe the same thing. The United States is willfully ceding its wealth, the rights of its citizens, and even its own national sovereignty to these supernational governmental entities. It's happening with stunning speed, and most people are blissfully unaware of the catastrophe.

FOUR

A DIFFERENT GOSPEL

It's natural to see the Antichrist as the chief villain of the end times, so people want to know about him. They often overlook his partner—the False Prophet. This character will, if anything, be even more treacherous, more vicious than his counterpart. Satan, the Antichrist, and the False Prophet will form an unholy trinity for the last days.

Diplomats, government planners, academics, and pundits almost always underestimate the power of religion in people's lives and actions. That's one reason the American military missions in Iraq and Afghanistan were so much more difficult than expected. People in those countries knew that welcoming Americans would be easier, and more profitable. Yet they fought against their own self-interest. They saw it as a religious duty. They did it for Islam.

After a century of down playing the power of religion's influence, the world's elite are now coming back to the idea of using it to manipulate the masses. They're beginning to understand that to control people, they must control people's religion. To unify and manipulate people, the Antichrist and False Prophet will provide them with a unifying and manipulating religion.

Understanding the power of religious faith, the "beasts" of Revelation will seize it for their own purposes. As the Bible's name for him implies, the False Prophet will be a religious leader. He will preside over a world unity religion. The Antichrist will be an object of faith and worship. That will be possible because the False Prophet will draw the world's religions into a single overarching faith.

Even today we hear that all religions at their heart, say the same thing, and all people worship the same God. It's absurd. It's an insult to each of those systems of faith. But Hollywood says it endlessly, as do those who place diversity above truth.

THE FALSE PROPHET

Revelation 13:11 introduces the False Prophet in a highly dramatic way. "Then I saw another beast coming up out of the earth, and he had two horns like a lamb and spoke like a dragon." We usually think of the Antichrist as "the beast." This verse shows that the False Prophet is also considered a beast.

"And he (the False Prophet) exercises all the authority of the first beast in his presence, and causes the earth and those who dwell in it to worship the first beast, whose deadly wound was healed. He performs great signs, so that he even makes fire come down from heaven on the earth in the sight of men. And he deceives those who dwell on the earth by those signs which he was granted to do in the sight of the beast, telling those who dwell on the earth to make an image to the beast who was wounded by the sword and lived" (Revelation 13:12-14).

In Revelation 13:3, we learned that the first beast, the Antichrist, will receive a deadly wound, yet live. It's reiterated here in verse 12. The False Prophet will make an image of the one who had this deadly wound.

"He (still speaking of the False Prophet) was granted power to give breath to the image of the beast, that the image of the beast should both speak and cause as many as would not worship the image of the beast to be killed" (Revelation 13:15).

In that day, those who refuse to worship the beast's image will be executed. It's something like the three Hebrew children being thrown into the furnace for not bowing down to King Nebuchadnezzar's image in Daniel 3.

LIKE A LAMB

A feel-good "spirituality" already permeates the thinking of most religious people. It centers around two things—the worship of creation and the social gospel.

Pope Francis often emphasizes his belief that social problems and environmental problems are related. In his encyclical on the environment, "Laudato Si," he said, "We are faced not with two separate crises, one environmental and the other social, but rather with one complex crisis, which is both social and environmental. Strategies for a solution demand an integrated approach to combating poverty, restoring dignity to the excluded and at the same time protecting nature."

The Antichrist will control the world through political machinations. The False Prophet will lead a world religion. And here's the important point—the religion will have a superficial resemblance to Christianity.

Look again at verse 11. "Then I saw another beast (the False Prophet) coming up out of the earth, and he had two horns like a lamb and spoke like a dragon" (Revelation 13:11).

When John the Baptist introduced Jesus, he said, "Behold! The Lamb of God who takes away the sin of the world!" (John 1:29). The False Prophet will also look like a lamb. He will have the outward appearance of Christ and Christianity.

THE SOCIAL GOSPEL

Looking like a good guy is an old trick for Satan and his children. 2 Corinthians 11:14 says, "Satan himself transforms himself into an angel of light."

Jesus said in John 8:44, "You are of your father the devil, and the desires of your father you want to do. He was a murderer from the beginning, and does not stand in the truth, because there is no truth in him. When he speaks a lie, he speaks from his own resources, for he is a liar and the father of it."

As the father of lies, he must be good at lying, as are his followers. The social gospel allows evil to masquerade in the garb of saints. It is Christianity minus Christ.

This story from John 12 will show you what I mean;

> Then, six days before the Passover, Jesus came to Bethany, where Lazarus was who had been dead, whom He had raised from the dead. There they made Him a supper; and Martha

served, but Lazarus was one of those who sat at the table with Him.

Then Mary took a pound of very costly oil of spikenard, anointed the feet of Jesus, and wiped His feet with her hair. And the house was filled with the fragrance of the oil. But one of His disciples, Judas Iscariot, Simon's son, who would betray Him, said, "Why was this fragrant oil not sold for three hundred denarii and given to the poor?"

This he said, not that he cared for the poor, but because he was a thief, and had the money box; and he used to take what was put in it. But Jesus said, "Let her alone; she has kept this for the day of My burial. For the poor you have with you always, but Me you do not have always" (John 12:1-8).

Later, Jesus called Judas "the son of perdition" (John 17:12). Only one other person in the entire Bible is called "the son of perdition" (2 Thessalonians 2:3). That is the Antichrist.

Judas pretended piety with his false outrage at Mary's gift. He looked very Christian. He seemed to be standing up for the poor. Hers was a sublime act of worship, but he proclaimed himself on the side of the kind of goodness that pulls on its boots and gets to work. He tried to make her act seem trivial compared to his own pragmatic care for the poor. He tried to make himself seem "holier than thou" (Isaiah 65:5 KJV).

That's the social gospel. It says, "You can keep your Jesus, but works come first. Go and do good things. Your good works will save you."

Jesus reversed that. He received her gift as an act of worship. The real gospel starts with Christ, and good works follow Him. In the last days religion, works will be everything. While some will maintain religious traditions that seem to honor Jesus, He will not be their life and breath. He will be just one more element in their cause—whatever that cause may be. But He will not be the cause at the heart of their lives.

The Bible depicts the False Prophet looking like a lamb. That means he will present himself in a way that reflects the popular conception of Jesus. But his words will reveal his true identity. He will speak like a dragon, like that old serpent called the Devil.

THE POPE'S GOSPEL

I'm not accusing Pope Francis of being the False Prophet. But he's giving us a glimpse of the False Prophet's theology and technique.

Francis has become a world leader in the ecology movement. In "Laudato Si," Pope Francis called for the "renewal of our relationship with nature." That doesn't make him a worshiper of nature, but it is another emphasis he shares with the coming False Prophet.

In May of 2013, Francis said, "The Lord has redeemed all of us, all of us, with the Blood of Christ: all of us, not just Catholics. Everyone! 'Father, the atheists?' Even the atheists. Everyone! And this Blood makes us children of God of the first class. We are created children in the likeness of God and the Blood of Christ has redeemed us all. And we all have a duty to do good. And this commandment for everyone to do good, I think, is a beautiful path towards peace. If we, each doing our own part, if we do good to others, if we meet there, doing good, and we go slowly, gently, little by little, we will make that culture of encounter: We need that so much. We must meet one another doing good. 'But I don't believe, Father, I am an atheist!' But do good: We will meet one another there."[6]

Many have reported that he said "all atheists will go to heaven." No. But he said something just as egregious. He said that good works will save even atheists.

---

6. "Pope at Mass: Culture of encounter is the foundation of peace," Vatican Radio, May 22, 2013, http://en.radiovaticana.va/storico/2013/05/22/pope_at_mass_culture_of_encounter_is_the_foundation_of_peace/en1-694445

In an article defending Francis, *Catholic Online* did a good job summing up the Pope's position. "He declared that all people, not just Catholics, are redeemed through Jesus, even atheists. However, he did emphasize there was a catch. Those people must still do good."

In other words, good works will save you. That's the social gospel. You don't have to believe. You don't have to accept the salvation of Jesus. Just do good. Rely on the goodness in your own heart.

If doing good saves us, then what good things should we do? Here's how Jesus answered the question. "Then they said to Him, 'What shall we do, that we may work the works of God?' Jesus answered and said to them, 'This is the work of God, that you believe in Him whom He sent'" (John 6:28-29).

You want to do the work of God? It starts with believing in Jesus.

After the famous John 3:16 verse, Jesus said, "For God did not send His Son into the world to condemn the world, but that the world through Him might be saved. He who believes in Him is not condemned; but he who does not believe is condemned already, because he has not believed in the name of the only begotten Son of God" (John 3:17-18).

By definition, the atheist "does not believe." You can trust the words of the Pope, or you can trust the words of Jesus Christ. Jesus said of the atheist, the one "who does not believe is condemned already."

OBAMA'S GOSPEL

After the Charleston Church shooting in June of 2015, President Obama, like most of us, was deeply moved by the victims' families' expressions of forgiveness toward the killer. According to the *Washington Post*, he later told members of his staff, "The essence of what is right about Christianity is embedded here.… They welcomed the stranger. They forgave the worst violence."

I appreciate the sentiment, but he got it completely turned around. Those miraculous attitudes were not the essence of what is right about Christianity. The welcoming and the forgiveness resulted from the real essence of Christianity, and that is Christ himself—His work on the cross, and His transforming power in our lives.

Jesus comes first, then comes good works and beautiful attitudes.

MOTHER TERESA'S GOSPEL

After Mother Teresa died, we learned some startling things about her. In a series of letters over a period of decades, she poured out her heart to a priest who served as her confessor. "Jesus has a very special love for you," she wrote. "As for me, the silence and the emptiness is so great, that I look and do not see,—Listen and do not hear—the tongue moves (in prayer) but does not speak."

At her confessor's suggestion, she wrote to God. "Lord, my God, who am I that You should forsake me? The Child of your Love—and now become as the most hated one— the one—You have thrown away as unwanted—unloved. I call, I cling, I want—and there is no One to answer— no One on Whom I can cling—no, No One.—Alone… Where is my Faith—even deep down right in there is nothing, but emptiness & darkness—My God—how painful is this unknown pain—I have no Faith—I dare not utter the words & thoughts that crowd in my heart—& make me suffer untold agony."[7]

That's just an example, but a representative one, of the hundreds of letters she wrote. Her "dark night of the soul" lasted for decades. There's no indication that her anguish toward God ever let up. The more success she had, the more people she helped, the more good she did, the more miserable she became.

7. "Mother Teresa as a Psalm," David Van Biema, September 2, 2012, https://www.washingtonpost.com/national/on-faith/mother-teresa-as-a-psalm/2012/09/07/3840885a-f909-11e1-a93b-7185e3f88849_story.html

There are many possible reasons why she was so miserable before God. The key may be in a statement she made to a group of political and business leaders in Washington, D.C. in 1989. She said, "We read in the gospel... 'Whatever you do to the least, my brethren, you did it to....'" Then she held up her hand and pointed to a finger for each word as she continued. "'You-did-it-to-Me.' Five fingers. The whole Gospel is in five fingers."

That's a beautiful verse, a glorious verse, but it's not "the whole Gospel." That verse is about works—doing things for Christ. As important as works are, we can't start there. Few in history worked harder, or did more good things than Mother Teresa. But on her own she could not be good enough, and she was miserable.

The social gospel fails in every way. It does not bring peace. It does not save. Even in the area of good works, it usually results in mere tokenism.

AFTER THE RAPTURE

Though not the False Prophet, Pope Francis shows us how the religious and political worlds are being prepared for the False Prophet and his religion. The stage is set and we're almost ready for the two leaders to make their entrance—Antichrist and his False Prophet; the political guy and the religious guy.

After the rapture of the church, it will all fall into place.

1 Thessalonians 4:16-17 says, "For the Lord Himself will descend from heaven with a shout, with the voice of an archangel, and with the trumpet of God. And the dead in Christ will rise first. Then we who are alive and remain shall be caught up together with them in the clouds to meet the Lord in the air."

The Greek word for "caught up" is *harpazo*. It literally means "to seize, to catch away." In Latin the word is *"rapturo."* That's where we get the word "rapture."

This is not the second coming because Christ never actually returns to the earth at the rapture. Instead, His people will "be caught up together…in the clouds to meet the Lord in the air."

As you can imagine, all true believers in Christ suddenly leaving the planet will cause an immediate and dramatic change in the state of affairs back on earth. At some point after the rapture—probably soon after—a seven year period known as "Daniel's 70th week" will begin.* The table has been set for the False Prophet. After the rapture, with Christians out of the way, the world will turn to his false religion.

---

*See Chapter eight for more details on Daniel's 70th week.

Then comes something totally unexpected. Right after the world's Christians disappear, new Christians will begin to appear. Even with strong delusion emanating from the new unity religion, after the rapture many will realize who Jesus is and what He has done. Of those who come to this realization, some will turn to Christ. At great cost to themselves and their families, they will become disciples of Jesus in the brave new world.

The one-world government and unity religion will see the new Christian believers as enemies of the state and of the unity faith. Initially, these Christians will do only limited damage to the New World Order because the Antichrist will be allowed to subdue them.

Revelation 13:7 says, "It was granted to him (the Antichrist) to make war with the saints and to overcome them."

FIVE

ILLUMINATI

Lured by possibilities of untold power and money, a host of organizations now exist whose goals are consistent with the creation of a New World Order. Some of these organizations have been working toward these goals for decades, perhaps even centuries.

Whatever faith the leaders of these groups once had in voters and legislative bodies is fast disappearing. Politics as usual, to them, is not working. In fact, they think uninformed and complacent voters are destroying the planet with a "me first" attitude. They see themselves and their fellow elites as the only hope to save Earth from the ravages of global warming and overpopulation.

Their model is oligarchy, not democracy. In an oligarchy, the elites run everything, or at least everything they want to run. Future oligarchs may present a facade of democracy to placate the masses, but they see taking power from the masses as essential for human survival on earth. In time they will appoint their men, the Antichrist and False Prophet, to unify the world.

I'm not talking about people in black robes worshiping Satan. These are highly accomplished, but otherwise regular people looking for ways to save the world. The catch is that they want to save humanity without turning to God. As I mentioned in Chapter 2, thoughtful men and women might reasonably question the effectiveness of democracy to fight the severe challenges facing the world. When they finally get behind the Antichrist and False Prophet, that too will seem reasonable. After all, these guys won't be wearing their biblical titles on their foreheads.

The new elites know that getting people to step away from the traditional beliefs of their forebears is difficult. The trick will be to make people think the new religion does no damage to the beliefs of established faiths. Even now, most people think that all religions, at their heart, are basically the same. The coming unity religion will make that part of its creed.

Real believers in Jesus, however, make a worldwide unity religion quite difficult. Christians committed to the authority of God's Word emphasize that Jesus is "the way, and the truth, and the life," and that no one comes to the Father, but through Him (John 14:6).

They speak of Jesus and say, "There is salvation in no one else; for there is no other name under heaven that has been given among men by which we must be saved" (Acts 4:12 NASB).

What do the New World Order people do to get rid of these troublesome Christ-followers? While mulling that problem, they will get a surprise they will find both terrifying and welcome. The ones they viewed as obstructionists, the Jesus people—will disappear.

THE CONSPIRATORS

For decades in locked rooms across the world, various groups have waited and planned for the opportunity that will be given to them in the chaos following the rapture. It's not that they expect the rapture, but they know a world cataclysm of some kind is inevitable. It might be anything from a virus to a volcanic eruption to a nuclear war. They know something big will eventually come along, and it will shake civilization to its foundations.

In the past, they worked incrementally, a little here and a little there. But after something as momentous as the rapture, the dominoes will start to fall, and the New World Order will rise quickly.

It's possible that the ten kings could come out of groups we already know about. Or it may not be any of these specific groups, but they will be like-minded people with vast wealth and influence. Let's look at a few.

ENLIGHTENED ONES

Conspiracy lovers love the Illuminati. It has everything. Imagine a secret organization that came into being just a couple of months before the United States issued the Declaration of Independence. Although new in terms of world history, from its inception the group claimed to possess secret knowledge from deep in prehistory.

The very word "Illuminati" seems to reflect the name Lucifer, or Satan in his guise as angel of light. And, while the name is known, the group remains secret. It has connections to freemasonry, to the French Revolution, and to global banking interests.

It's a veritable feast of conspiracy possibilities, but with roots in known history. There are real things we know about the Illuminati, but more that we don't know. Conspiracy buffs love it because the known facts are tantalizing, while leaving room for infinite imagination.

Here are the basic facts. First, the Illuminati is real. It did not spring forth from the imagination of a Hollywood screenwriter. There really was a secret Bavarian group called the Illuminati established in 1776. Its founder,

Adam Weishaupt, initially claimed to have secret knowledge and rituals passed down from humanity's distant past. We now know he lied about that. He and his closest colleagues made up the rituals and beliefs as they went along.

The group did not have roots in prehistory. It arose during a period in European and American history known as "the Enlightenment"—thus the name. "Illuminati" is the plural form of the Latin word meaning "enlightened." It means "enlightened ones."

Adam Weishaupt served as the only non-clerical professor at a Jesuit-run university, and became an embittered critic of the clergy. Under his leadership, the Illuminati became deeply immersed in 18th century rationalism. Like H. G. Wells and so many others, they dreamed of a government built on reason, run by philosophers and scientists.

PERFECTIBILISTS ENLIST THE MASONS

Before calling the group, "The Illuminati," Weishaupt called it "the Covenant of Perfectibility." Most people called them "Perfectibilists." It was a form of what we would call humanism. It placed man at the center of the universe, discounting God. A perfectibilist believed in the ability of man to perfect himself.

In writing about the Illuminati founder, Thomas Jefferson said, "Weishaupt (sic) seems to be an enthusiastic Philanthropist. He is among those... who believe in the indefinite perfectibility of man. He thinks he may in time be rendered so perfect that he will be able to govern himself in every circumstance so as to injure none, to do all the good he can, to leave government no occasion to exercise their powers over him, & of course to render political government useless."

From the beginning, Weishaupt patterned the Illuminati after the Freemasons. Later, the Illuminati formed their own masonic lodge.

Scholars have a variety of opinions as to their real purpose. At times, they just seemed to want growth for its own sake. They claimed to be for equal rights, but their own society was exceedingly hierarchical. While claiming to stand up for the common man, they showed a distinct preference for adding members with titles and money. The bigger the title, the faster a man rose in their ranks.

In 1784, Bavaria's ruler, Charles Theodore, outlawed the Illuminati at the urging of the Catholic Church. They came to see the group in much the same way as conspiracy theorists see it today. They believed the Illuminati was intent on the overthrow of governments, and the creation of a new order.

In a letter to Illuminati leaders, Weishaupt wrote, "Do you realize sufficiently what it means to rule—to rule in a secret society? Not only over the lesser or more important of the populace, but over the best of men, over men of all ranks, nations, and religions, to rule without external force, to unite them indissolubly, to breathe one spirit and soul into them, men distributed over all parts of the world?"[8]

Some conspiracists say that at the Freemasons 1782 Congress of Wilhelmsbad, the masons put Weishaupt in charge of creating a one-world government. Did this happen? We can only speculate. One man who attended the conference, Comte de Virieu, ended his association with freemasonry over something that happened at the conference. One person claimed to have asked de Virieu his reasons for breaking with the group. He claimed that Comte de Virieu answered, "I will not confide them to you. I can only tell you that all this is very much more serious than you think."

Tantalizing, but far from certain.

ROTHSCHILD AND REVOLUTION

We also have evidence that Weishaupt forged an alliance with the Rothschild banking network. So what did

8. "Greeting to the newly integrated illuminatos dirigentes", in Nachtrag von weitern Originalschriften vol. 2 (1787) p. 45.

the Illuminati do with all this power? We don't know. It's a secret. But there are some intriguing hints.

In the last few years, new evidence has arisen confirming a suspicion held at the time of the French Revolution, that Illuminati members were influential in that uprising. They were not the primary cause, but they were among the instigators.

Don't think of the French Revolution as France's version of the American revolution. Both addressed "the rights of man," but Americans saw those rights as an endowment from the Creator. The French believed human rights arose from "Reason," not God. In fact, the French Revolution struck out at God as much as it did against tyranny. The revolutionaries tried to de-Christianize all of France—ransacking churches, criminalizing public worship, confiscating church lands, destroying crosses, while executing and imprisoning priests and other clergy.

The revolutionary government instituted a new religion to replace Christianity. They called it "The Cult of Reason." They transformed Notre Dame Cathedral into the "Temple of Reason." Historian Barr Ferree wrote, "The orgies of pagan Rome did not surpass in vindictiveness and debauchery those newly-made pagans of the

Revolution perpetrated in the holy places of Christian religion."[9]

In the beginning, actresses and ballerinas played the role of "goddess of reason" in temple ceremonies, but, according to Edmund de Pressence, as public enthusiasm waned, the leaders tried "to reanimate the fervor by replacing actresses with prostitutes."[10] Jetta Sophia Wolff wrote, "The church became a place of rioting and debauchery."[11]

Present-day historians sometimes downplay such vileness, but those who wrote about the events at the time emphasized the lascivious nature of the movement. Though the revolutionaries worshiped reason, their actions were anything but reasonable. They executed over 41,000 people in less than a year, 16,000 of them by guillotine. We remember it as "the Reign of Terror" for good reason.

MEN LOVED DARKNESS RATHER THAN LIGHT

I'm not blaming all of this on the Illuminati, but secret organizations including the Illuminati played a huge role.

9. *The Cathedrals of France* by Barr Ferree
10. *Religion and the Reign of Terror: Or, the Church During the French Revolution* by Edmund de Pressence. https://archive.org/stream/religionreignoft00pres_0/religionreignoft00pres_0_djvu.txt
11. *The Story of the Paris Churches* by Jetta Sophia Wolff

Jacobin Clubs were a French secret organization until they grew too large to remain a secret. Today, no one doubts the central role the Jacobins played in the revolution.

Secret societies are a bad idea. Jesus meant for the church to be an open institution. Of course, some things must be confidential. Church bulletins don't give details on who went to pastors for counseling or why. But the church must never teach "secret knowledge." It must be up front and in the open—just like Jesus.

After His arrest outside the garden of Gethsemane, the soldiers took Jesus to the high priest. "The high priest then asked Jesus about His disciples and His doctrine. Jesus answered him, 'I spoke openly to the world. I always taught in synagogues and in the temple, where the Jews always meet, and in secret I have said nothing. Why do you ask Me? Ask those who have heard Me what I said to them. Indeed they know what I said'" (John 18:19-21).

Jesus taught openly. So must we.

While Jesus did have private teaching sessions with his closest disciples, He told them this. "Whatever I tell you in the dark, speak in the light; and what you hear in the ear, preach on the housetops" (Matthew 10:27).

Humanity is bent toward secrecy because its deeds are evil. Even those who call themselves "enlightened," prefer to keep their actions hidden in darkness.

In John 3:19-21, Jesus said, "This is the condemnation, that the light has come into the world, and men loved darkness rather than light, because their deeds were evil. For everyone practicing evil hates the light and does not come to the light, lest his deeds should be exposed. But he who does the truth comes to the light, that his deeds may be clearly seen, that they have been done in God."

ILLUMI-NUTS

Today, lots of secret groups call themselves "The Illuminati." Most of them should not be taken seriously. They're simply adults playing a game of pretend. They are powerless people deluding themselves into believing they have some influence over world events. Such people would have infinitely more access to power by simply falling on their knees in prayer.

While we know the Illuminati was once an order within Freemasons, and later kicked out, we don't know if reports of their current cooperation are true. Even if they are, we cannot conclude that every mason is part of the Illuminati. Some people have gone crazy with this stuff.

For instance, some of them say that America is just one big Illuminati conspiracy. They point to the configuration of streets in Washington, D.C. as channeling some kind of satanic power. They point out that George Washington and several other founding fathers were masons. They ignore the fact that George Washington loved the Lord, and condemned the Illuminati.

In a 1798 letter to George Synder, Washington wrote, "I have heard much of the nefarious, and dangerous plan, and doctrines of the Illuminati.... I believe notwithstanding, that none of the Lodges in this Country are contaminated with the principles ascribed to the Society of the Illuminati."

A month later, he wrote again to Synder hoping to correct what he perceived to be a misunderstanding. "It was not my intention to doubt that, the Doctrines of the Illuminati, and principles of Jacobinism had not spread in the United States. On the contrary, no one is more truly satisfied of this fact than I am.

"The idea that I meant to convey, was, that I did not believe that the Lodges of Free Masons in this Country had, as Societies, endeavored to propagate the diabolical tenets of the first, or pernicious principles of the latter (if they are susceptible of separation). That Individuals of them may have done it, or that the founder, or instrument employed to found, the Democratic Societies in the United States, may have had these objects; and actually had a separation of the People from their Government in view, is too evident to be questioned."

Washington was a mason, but heartily condemned the Illuminati. So be careful about blanket statements. "My cousin is part of the Masons, so he must be of the devil." No. It doesn't work that way.

Most masons are not knowingly working toward a one-world government. The Illuminati may or may not be a viable organization working today. But we know with certainty that scores of organizations working for a one-world government do exist. Some of them are connected to the highest seats of power.

In his novel, *Captains and Kings*, Taylor Caldwell tells of an immigrant who became successful in the United States. The underlying theme was that the really powerful people in Washington are not the politicians, but the super rich who buy politicians.

History abounds with small groups successfully conspiring to create big and lasting changes. It's happening again right now.

SIX

SHADOW GOVERNMENT

The World Economic Forum founded in 1971 brings business, academic, and government leaders together. They have become a government think tank for the world, even though there is nothing official about them. WEF is a private nonprofit organization headquartered in Cologny, Switzerland. Who elected them to this leadership role? The elites elected themselves.

There are many, many others.

The Federal Reserve began in 1913; the League of Nations lasted from 1920 to 1946; the Council on Foreign Relations was founded in 1921; and the United Nations in 1945. The European Union began with the Treaty of Rome in 1958 and took its present form with the Maastricht Treaty in 1993, shortly after the fall of the Iron Curtain.

The Ancient and Accepted Scottish Rite of Freemasonry traces its roots to a lodge in London in 1733. People describing themselves as "a group of world citizens, sharing a common concern for the future of humanity" founded the Club of Rome in 1968. David Rockefeller founded the Trilateral Commission in 1973.

BILDERBERG

The Bilderberg Group, formed in 1954, brings together Americans and Europeans for a highly secretive annual meeting. Just because someone has attended a Bilderberg meeting does not mean he or she favors a one-world government. However, that is the general thrust of the group as a whole.

Like the others, Bilderberg is highly secretive. For decades, there was no press coverage of them at all. Today, that coverage is minimal. Participants are sworn to secrecy, ostensibly so that the leaders can speak their mind without fear. But that really doesn't hold water. They're speaking their mind to the most influential people in the world. They're not afraid of being heard or disagreed with. They fear what the public will think if it learns about their real beliefs and agenda.

A few years ago, British politician Denis Healey gave us a glimpse of that agenda. Healey helped found the group back in 1954, and served on the steering committee for thirty years. He said, "To say we were striving for a one-world government is exaggerated, but not wholly unfair. Those of us in Bilderberg felt we couldn't go on forever fighting one another for nothing and killing people and rendering millions homeless. So we felt that a single community throughout the world would be a good thing."

One of Bilderberg's stated goals is the promotion of capitalism but as China proves, a capitalistic financial system does not guarantee a representative form of government. For the Bilderberg Group, it's all about bringing money and power to the elites. They think they can make more money with a one-world system than with the system we have now.

They also want to reserve power for themselves. Earlier I mentioned that these groups model themselves on oligarchy, not democracy. It's evident in the way Bilderberg conducts its meetings. Just to merit an invitation requires political power, great wealth, or great acclaim. It is the definition of elitism.

SUPERNATIONAL SOVEREIGNTY

After the Bilderberg Group's meeting in Germany in 1991, several French newspapers began running a David Rockefeller quote they said had been leaked to them from that year's meeting.

We are grateful to the *Washington Post*, the *New York Times*, *Time Magazine* and other great publications whose directors have attended our meetings and respected their promises of discretion for almost forty years.... It would have been impossible for us to develop our plan for the world if we had been subjected to the lights of publicity during those years. But, the world is more sophisticated and prepared to march towards a world government. The supernational sovereignty of an intellectual elite and world bankers is surely preferable to the national autodetermination* practiced in past centuries.

If he really said it, we can see why they shroud their meetings in such secrecy. Here's what we know. The leaders of major news organizations have been present for the meetings. With only minor exceptions, they have never reported on the proceedings, although such information is certainly newsworthy.

The shroud of secrecy has, as the Rockefeller quotation suggests, allowed them to make plans that would have ruined their business and political careers were those plans made public. We also know that a "supernational

---

*French for "self-determination"

sovereignty of an intellectual elite" has been their major thrust during the years of the group's existence.

We also know, as the quote suggests, that they are increasingly leery of national self-determination. Rockefeller apparently used the word "autodetermination" which means the same thing.

They believe in capitalism, yet view democracy as a mere tool for keeping the masses in line. It makes the people feel they have a voice. But elites such as these work to make sure the "right people" get elected. Of course, democracy is messy, and sometimes the "wrong people" get into office. When that happens, Bilderberg-type people don't panic. They simply woo these newly elected people by giving them a taste of real power. Before you know it, they've turned "wrong people" into "right people."

At heart, elites do not believe members of the general public should make big decisions for mankind. If they did, they would open their meetings to press coverage, and they would invite someone other than their fellow elites to join the discussion.

With good reason, they see the electorate as ill-informed and easily manipulated. While keeping a facade of democracy, several organizations of world elites—not just Bilderberg—are consolidating power. Though perhaps none of them yet see it as their long term plan, they will eventually consolidate their power into the ten kings of Revelation 17.

FEDERAL RESERVE

When we begin to study the proponents of globalism, we have to be careful not to be what the Bible calls a "tale-bearer." It is important to try to separate truth from fiction, and when it comes to conspiracies, that's not easy. We have to ask how so many conspiracy theorists know the contents of secret conversations held decades, sometimes centuries ago.

Staying within the known evidence, we still see the ultra-rich protecting their positions. It's consistent with human nature. We could go into depth here on the Council on Foreign Relations, the Federal Reserve, and other organizations. Suffice it to say, people with money and influence usually work to protect and expand both.

And they're not above trickery and manipulation. Look at the name "Federal Reserve." Most people hear that and think it is part of the federal government of the United States. In fact, it is neither federal nor a reserve. It is a privately held corporation. Stockholders include some of the world's most influential banks owned by the world's moneyed elite.

Today, the Federal Reserve may be the most powerful non-governmental entity in the world. It controls how much money the U.S. will print and the interest rates at which it will be loaned. That gives the major power players of the Federal Reserve an incredible level of influence over all our lives.

RIDER ON A BLACK HORSE

Now look at it in light of Revelation. "When He opened the third seal, I heard the third living creature say, 'Come and see.' So I looked, and behold, a black horse, and he who sat on it had a pair of scales in his hand. And I heard a voice in the midst of the four living creatures saying, 'A quart of wheat for a denarius, and three quarts of barley for a denarius; and do not harm the oil and the wine'" (Revelation 6:5-6).

The rider on the black horse represents economic collapse. When this rider gallops through the world, the global economy will tank. It will collapse. A denarius represents a day's pay. That means food will be scarce. The scales demonstrate that bread, and other basic foods, will be weighed out as carefully as gold.

A voice tells the rider of the black horse, "Do not harm the oil and the wine." Those were luxury items in the first century. The rider on the black horse will not harm the super rich, but will destroy the middle class.

In America today, obesity has become a major problem among the poor. That's a unique circumstance in history. But in the days of the black horse, getting enough food will be tough for anyone other than the extremely wealthy. The poor in those days will work a full day for just enough to feed their family that one day. And almost everyone will be poor.

We see the beginning of it today. The middle class is failing—not just in America, but around the world. Meanwhile, the ultra-wealthy are becoming fantastically rich beyond anything ever seen before.

THE CLUB OF ROME

Aurelio Peccei, an Italian industrialist, and Alexander King, a Scottish scientist, established the Club of Rome in 1968. As you might guess from the name, the Club of Rome was formed in the city of Rome.

Revelation 17:9 mentions a city with seven hills. (The King James and New King James Versions say "mountains," but the Greek word literally means "a rise." That fits a hill or a mountain.) Since ancient times, Rome has been famous as "the city on seven hills."

The Club of Rome is an environmentalist think tank and consultant group to the United Nations. In 1972, it released *The Limits to Growth*,[12] a book on the dangers of overpopulation. According to the Club's official website, "12 million copies were distributed in 37 languages."

In 1989, Ronald Bailey, science editor of *Forbes Magazine*, looked back on the book and laughed. He said it was "as wrong-headed as it is possible to be.... *Limits to Growth* predicted that at 1972 rates of growth the world would run out of gold by 1981, mercury by 1985, tin by 1987, zinc by 1990, petroleum by 1992, copper, lead and natural gas by 1993."

During the years immediately after the book's release, it was a roaring success. It changed the world's conversation on matters of population and the environment. Later, when the predictions started falling apart, the Club of Rome tried to say they were not really predictions at all. They said the book was simply laying out possible scenarios.

According to public Club of Rome documents, the really dire things predicted by the book will not take place until well into the twenty-first century. But even a cursory examination proves that the book did in fact predict all the things Bailey said including the end of the world's natural gas supply by 1993.

---

12. *Limits to Growth* by Donella H. Meadows, Jorgen Randers & Dennis L. Meadows.

The book predicted a grim twentieth century for the earth. Its urgent tone can be seen from the beginning. It starts with a 1969 quotation from U Thant, Secretary-General of the United Nations from 1961 to 1971.

"I do not wish to seem overdramatic," U Thant said, "but I can only conclude from the information that is available to me as Secretary-General, that the members of the United Nations have perhaps ten years left in which to subordinate their ancient quarrels and launch a global partnership to curb the arms race, to improve the human environment, to defuse the population explosion, and to supply the required momentum to development efforts. If such a global partnership is not forged within the next decade, then I very much fear that the problems I have mentioned will have reached such staggering proportions that they will be beyond our capacity to control."

You can't read that quote at the beginning of a book and think its warnings are for fifty or a hundred years later. In 1969, he said, "within the next decade."

In 1991, the Club of Rome published a book titled, *The First Global Revolution*.[13] "In searching for a common enemy against whom we can unite," they wrote, "we came up

---

13. Alexander King & Bertrand Schneider, *The First Global Revolution* (New York: Pantheon Books, 1991).

with the idea that pollution, the threat of global warming, water shortages, famine and the like, would fit the bill.... All these dangers are caused by human intervention in natural processes, and it is only through changed attitudes and behavior that they can be overcome. The real enemy then is humanity itself."

Like Nimrod of ancient times, they looked for a way to unite mankind under a one-world government. Instead of a tower to unite us, the Club of Rome chose to use a common enemy. The enemy involved pollution, the threat of global warming, water shortages, and famine, but as they finally admitted, "The real enemy then is humanity itself."

WIELDING THE VATICAN'S SWORD

Club of Rome member, Hans Schellnhuber, serves as the Pope's primary climate adviser. *The National Catholic Register* says, "The climatologist and self-professed atheist was involved from the beginning to the conclusion of *Laudato Si.*"

In a talk given to the 2009 Copenhagen Climate Change Conference, Hans-Joachim Schellnhuber said, "In a very cynical way, it's a triumph for science because at last we have stabilized something—namely the estimates for the carrying capacity of the planet, namely below 1 billion people." At that population level, he said there would be "no fluctuations anymore, we can be fairly sure."

In 2015, he became a member of the Pontifical Academy of Sciences. As a Vatican insider, he naturally denies calling for population controls. But we can see from the above quote that he believes reducing earth's population from 7.4 billion to 1 billion would bring environmental problems under control.

He has openly called for a one-world government with an "Earth Constitution," a "Global Council," and a "Planetary Court." He explains them like this. The "Earth Constitution would transcend the UN Charter and identify those first principles guiding humanity in its quest for freedom, dignity, security and sustainability. The Global Council would be an assembly of individuals elected directly by all people on Earth, where eligibility should be not constrained by geographical, religious, or cultural quotas; and the Planetary Court would be a transnational legal body open to appeals from everybody, especially with respect to violations of the Earth Constitution."

In a study titled, "Geocybernetics: Controlling a Complex Dynamical System Under Uncertainty," he wrote, "While the borders of nation states have become almost irrelevant to global economic players (for instance) after the end of the Cold War, human and natural rights are still confined and dominated by thousands of frontiers. This situation can only be overcome by giving up a good deal of national sovereignty and establishing a true regime of global governance. As a prerequisite, the rather symbolic parts and pieces of the UN system must be transformed into powerful supra-national institutions: allons corriger le futur!"[14]

"Allons corriger le futur" is French for "will fix the future."

So, how do we "fix the future?" Nations must give up "a good deal of national sovereignty." They must establish "a true regime of global governance," and transform the UN into a "powerful supra-national institution."

CONSPIRACY?

This is not a wild-eyed conspiracy theory. Hans Schellnhuber exists. He is one of the most influential men in the world, and he really said the things I've quoted. He's a close advisor to German Chancellor Angela Merkel. Schellnhuber has become the Pope's leading advisor on climate change, something near to the Pope's heart. Both he and the Pope see global governance as the best solution for the future of humanity and the planet.

---

14. Hans-Joachim Schellnhuber, Jürgen Kropp, *Geocybernetics: Controlling a Rather Complex Dynamical System Under Uncertainty* (Potsdam: Potsdam Inst. for Climate Impact Research, 1998).

Though the Vatican, the Club of Rome, and the Bilderberg Group are clearly working toward a world government, they would not call it a conspiracy. They would call it "problem solving." To them, a one-world government is a practical requirement for the long-term survival of humanity.

Conspiring? Of course not. They would say they are planning. Yes, getting together in secret conclaves to do their planning might sound conspiratorial to the average person, but they see themselves well above Mr. or Ms. Average.

Do any of them actually worship Satan? Do any of them believe they are bringing about the rise of the Antichrist? While such dark believers may exist, there are few. Elites don't need to be satanic conspirators, or James Bond villains. They are helping to bring about conditions described in Bible prophecy, and they have no idea. Their participation in this endtimes cabal only requires that they believe a supernational world government is the best answer for what the Club of Rome calls "the predicament of mankind." They see themselves as pragmatists in white hats.

The elites don't know it, but a real satanic conspiracy exists. How satanic is it? It's run by Satan himself. He and his demonic minions have been conspiring for a long time. They have vast influence among those who reject the God of the Bible, but not because these people worship Satan. The key to his influence over most of them is that they know nothing about him. Elites who imagine themselves masters of the world have become pawns in a battle about which they have no conception.

SEVEN

GOG DRAWN SOUTH

America has intriguing relationships with all the nations and regions the Bible identifies as significant players in the end times. By looking at those relationships, we can see a panorama of Bible prophecies for the last days, and get a good idea about America's future.

Ezekiel 38 and 39 are among the most familiar passages of Bible prophecy. Chapter 38 begins, "Now the word of the Lord came to me, saying, 'Son of man, set your face against Gog, of the land of Magog, the prince of Rosh, Meshech, and Tubal, and prophesy against him'" (Ezekiel 38:1-2).

Verse 1 shows that Gog is a person. In Ezekiel 38:14 and 39:1, God addresses him as an individual. He's a leader. In verses 38:2 and 39:1, he's called a "prince." Magog, on the other hand, is a nation. We know that because the scripture says, "Gog, of the land of Magog." So Gog is the leader of Magog—maybe a king or president.

AMERICA IN THE NEW WORLD ORDER

There are both secular and biblical reasons to identify Magog as Russia. Since it's not our focus here, we
won't go into detail on those reasons. But let me give one.
Ezekiel 38:6, 15, and 39:2 all refer to these lands as "the
far north"—not just "the north," but "the far north."

Get a globe or a map, find Israel and then look to the
"far north." What do you see? Russia.

Ezekiel wrote the names of the regions as they were
known then. Magog, Rosh, Meshech, and Tubal represent
areas within the former Soviet Union extending south as
far as Turkey.

> "Thus says the Lord God: 'Behold, I am against
> you, O Gog, the prince of Rosh, Meshech, and
> Tubal. I will turn you around, put hooks into
> your jaws, and lead you out, with all your army,
> horses, and horsemen, all splendidly clothed, a
> great company with bucklers and shields, all of
> them handling swords'" (Ezekiel 38:3-4).

In modern terms, this means the army will be well-
equipped, mechanized, and highly mobile.

GOG'S ALLIES

Verses 5 and 6 give a list of nations allied under Gog's
leadership. It starts with Persia, which we can easily

identify. Today, most people outside the country call it Iran, but the nation has officially said that either name, Iran or Persia, is correct and acceptable to them. Persia is their name from antiquity.

I've met a lot of people who are from Iran. I've ministered with people from Iran, and in outreach to the country. Ask somebody from Iran, "Are you Iranian?" and they will say, "No, I am Persian."

BROUGHT OUT OF THE NATIONS

Verse 8 is still speaking to the Russian leader, Gog. "After many days you will be visited. In the latter years you will come into the land of those brought back from the sword and gathered from many people on the mountains of Israel, which had long been desolate; they were brought out of the nations, and now all of them dwell safely" (Ezekiel 38:8).

"The latter years" refers to the last days, the time just before the return of Jesus.

It speaks next of the Jews returning to the land of Israel. Since the time of Joshua, Israelites have always been present in the holy land. But starting around 2,500 years ago, most of them began to be scattered around the world, just as the prophets had foretold. Then, about 150 years ago, for a host of reasons, they began to return—at first a trickle, and then a flood.

In 1948, Israel once again became a country, and even more Jews immigrated to the land. In the last couple of years, increased European anti-Semitism caused a new wave of Jewish migration back to the land of their fathers.

God said to Gog, "In future years you will invade a land that has recovered from war, whose people were gathered from many nations to the mountains of Israel, which had long been desolate. They had been brought out from the nations…" (Ezekiel 38:8 NIV).

For two millennia, those conditions did not exist in Israel. Now they do.

However, the next phrase has not happened yet. It says, "and now all of them live in safety" (Ezekiel 38:8 NIV).

That won't happen until Israel signs a peace treaty with the Antichrist (Daniel 9:27). That treaty will trigger the beginning of Daniel's 70th week.* Many of the calamities you've read in prophecy, including the worldwide upheavals described in Revelation, will begin when Antichrist breaks his treaty with Israel three-and-one-half years after signing it.

---

*See Chapter eight for more details on Daniel's 70th week.

MAGOG INVADES

Verse 9 speaks again to Gog, the ruler of Russia who will lead this confederacy of nations;

> You and all your troops and the many nations with you will go up, advancing like a storm; you will be like a cloud covering the land. This is what the Sovereign Lord says: "On that day thoughts will come into your mind and you will devise an evil scheme. You will say, 'I will invade a land of unwalled villages; I will attack a peaceful and unsuspecting people—all of them living without walls and without gates and bars. I will plunder and loot and turn my hand against the resettled ruins and the people gathered from the nations, rich in livestock and goods, living at the center of the land'" (Ezekiel 38:9-12 NIV).

"Livestock and goods" means that the Jews gathered again in Israel will have acquired great wealth. The land that was barren will be fruitful, and they will dwell in the midst of the land. That is happening today. Israel has become a world leader in computer and other high technology industries. They developed sophisticated irrigation techniques that have become the envy of other nations, allowing the desert to bloom.

In a *Forbes Magazine* article, Steve Forbes called it "the miracle of the Israeli economy." He said, "With the exception of the U.S., Israel—a country of a mere 8 million people—leads the world in high tech, an astonishing feat." He also noted that "Israeli milk cows are the world's most productive," and that "this desert nation solved its water crisis."[15]

Even with all that, what specifically will Russia seek to plunder? Golda Meir used to joke that God gave the Jewish people the only land in the Middle East without oil. However, in the last few years, Israeli companies have discovered two massive gas fields off their coast in the Mediterranean Sea. There are 30 trillion cubic feet of known gas reserves in those two fields. The U.S. Geological Survey estimates more than twice that amount remains to be discovered in Israeli waters. Perhaps those gas fields will entice the Russian leader to move against Israel.

In December of 2015, Israeli Prime Minister Benjamin Netanyahu said, "The gas was given to us as a gift from God, found in the deep sea, where we were given enormous gas reserves. They potentially transform us not just into an energy power, but certainly into an important

---

15. Steve Forbes, "How the Small State of Israel Is Becoming A High-Tech Superpower," *Forbes*, July 22, 2015.

international energy force with a very great capability—and we need to extract them."

> "Sheba, Dedan, the merchants of Tarshish, and all their young lions will say to you, 'Have you come to take plunder? Have you gathered your army to take booty, to carry away silver and gold, to take away livestock and goods, to take great plunder?'" (Ezekiel 38:13).

They will say, "Have you come to ransack and loot?" Gas, oil, high technology, industrial secrets, new methods of desalinization, whatever it may be—"Have you come to take it?"

RUSSIA ON THE DOORSTEP

Syria stands on Israel's northeast border, along the area known as the Golan Heights. In the fall of 2015, Russia moved a large, highly mechanized military force into Syria. Russian President Vladimir Putin made the move in an attempt to bolster Syrian President Bashar al-Assad in the Syrian civil war. Putin's Syrian operation came at the request of Russia's ally, Iran, also a staunch supporter of Assad.

Putin publicly claimed to have gone into Syria to fight ISIS. From the moment of their first sorties, however, the

Russians made it clear that they were gunning for any Syrians who opposed President Assad.

In March of 2016, Russia announced a partial pull out of Syria. President Putin said they were leaving because, "I consider the mission set for the Defense Ministry and the armed forces on the whole has been accomplished."

Mission accomplished? When Russia "left" Syria, ISIS and al-Qaeda were approximately as strong as when they arrived. The Russian's real damage was to schools, civilians, and the so-called "moderate rebels" allied with the United States.

From a prophetic standpoint, two things about this situation stand out. First, the two main leaders of the Ezekiel 38 coalition, Russia and Iran, have become inextricably linked, and it happened recently. They are now committed to each other, body and soul. Second, despite Russia's partial pull-out, they're keeping the Khmeimim airbase and the Mediterranean port at Tartus. That means they will maintain their military infrastructure in Syria. Iran will, too.

The Bible says these two nations will one day lead a massive coalition in an overwhelming attack on Israel. And both have now established a major stepping stone that sits on Israel's northern border.

Look again at God's words to Gog in Ezekiel 38:4. "I will turn you around, put hooks into your jaws, and lead you out, with all your army, horses, and horsemen, all splendidly clothed."

All these armies are coming. The alliances are forming right now. They will come from Turkey, Russia, Iran, and certain African nations. Syria makes a perfect staging area for an assault on Israel.

DAMASCUS

Civil war has all but destroyed everything in Syria except one city—Damascus. The Syrian capital may be the oldest continuously inhabited city in the world. It is certainly the oldest that has never been destroyed. This is fascinating because Isaiah 17 prophesied specifically about Damascus. Isaiah said Damascus will be obliterated in a single night.

Isaiah 17:1 says, "Behold, Damascus will cease from being a city, and it will be a ruinous heap." And it gets worse. Isaiah 17:14 says, "Behold, at eventide, trouble! And before the morning, he is no more."

Damascus covers a small area for such a large population. Over 1.7 million people live there, and it covers an area of only about 40 square miles. Phoenix, Arizona has a smaller population—1.5 million—but covers 517 square miles. Damascus has twice the population density of New York, which has by far the highest population density among U.S. cities.

The small footprint of Damascus makes it easier to intellectually grasp how it could be destroyed in a few hours, especially in an era of nuclear warfare. But the large population makes it emotionally unthinkable. So far, Damascus has remained eerily untouched by the Syrian civil war raging around it. Damascus suburbs have been blown to pieces, but not the city itself.

WHY RUSSIA TURNS SOUTH

God will draw Gog toward Israel as if he were a big fish or large animal. "I will turn you around, put hooks into your jaws, and lead you out" (Ezekiel 38:4).

In 2014, Russia invaded, then annexed Crimea. In simple terms, they stole Crimea from Ukraine. Though vast, Russia remains mostly landlocked. Their large naval base in Crimea gives them their best access to the Black Sea, and from there, the oceans of the world.

Will Russia make a push into Europe? Putin seems to be testing the waters in Ukraine and several other former nations of the Soviet Union. While political leaders in the

United States and Europe show no great resolve to stop them, NATO has quietly amassed a large arsenal, building up its forces, and creating supply lines in Eastern Europe.

Will Russian aggression finally shake the NATO nations out of their complacency? When Russia meets real resistance in Eastern Europe, will it look for easier pickings? Will NATO resistance be the thing that turns Russia around?

Russia seems to be thinking in these terms already. Invading Israel would make Russia extremely popular with its Muslim allies. Also, with a faltering economy, Russia is desperate for an influx of goods and cash, i.e., "plunder and loot."

That makes the Israeli gas fields in the Mediterranean a fascinating plot twist. Russia supplies a quarter of Europe's natural gas. Demand there seems certain to go up, despite fears of climate change. But environmentalists have strong sway in Europe, and they won't allow the continent to tap its own petroleum reserves through fracking and other techniques. This allows Russia to charge Europe exorbitant fees for its gas. It's one of the few bright spots in Russia's otherwise bleak economic outlook.

Israel's Eastern Mediterranean gas fields could dramatically change the equation. Russia's position is so strong in

Europe that Europeans pay $2\frac{1}{2}$ times the amount paid by Americans. Competition would bring that down dramatically. To hedge its bets, Russia's state-owned Gazprom energy company has a deal in place to market Israeli liquified natural gas.

While Israel has vast gas reserves offshore, they don't have the infrastructure needed to take full advantage of the new finds. They're building that infrastructure, but it is highly vulnerable to terrorism. Vladimir Putin has assured Israel that if Gazprom receives a stake in their gas, he will guarantee the security of the fields and help with the needed infrastructure.

To Putin, it's like chess. By putting his military into Syria, he has positioned himself for a lightning strike if things don't go as he wants. From Syria, his forces can move on Israeli gas fields within minutes of him giving the order. Putin may not always wear a shirt, but he's been on the world scene a long time. He knows how to play the game.

THE SUNNI-SHIITE DIVIDE

The Muslim world consists of two main factions— Sunnis and Shiites. The Sunnis make up between 85 and 90 percent of Muslims, leaving the Shiites with 10 to 15 percent. Saudi Arabia is Sunni. Iran is Shiite, sometimes called "Shia."

Sunnis have one eschatology (belief about the way events will unfold in the last days), and the Shiites have another. Sunnis are usually the ones strapping bombs around themselves and wreaking some kind of terror. The terrorist organizations of ISIS, al-Qaeda, and Hamas are Sunni. Sunni Muslims, primarily from Saudi Arabia, planned and executed the 9/11 terror attacks on the United States.

Shiite understanding of the last days centers around bringing back the Mahdi, a sort of Islamic messiah. Sunnis also believe in a Mahdi, but they don't see his role in the same way. Shiites believe he will return at a time of worldwide chaos.

It's true that Christians believe Jesus will return at a time of great conflict and trial, but the circumstances described by the Bible are utterly beyond human manipulation. Shiites are willing to create an apocalypse to hurry the Mahdi's return. Christians sit back and marvel as we see God fulfill His Word. Shiite Muslims think their prophecies need some help to come true.

They want to create a fiery disaster to force the Mahdi's return. A desire for chaos drives Iran's quest for nuclear weapons. That's why it's so important that they never get such weapons. To other nations, nuclear war is unthinkable. To the radicals running Iran, nuclear war is a moral imperative! Their apocalyptic ideology absolutely justifies first-use of nuclear weapons.

We don't hear of Iranian suicide bombers. Shiite Iran sees a much grander picture than bombing buses. That's why they are allies with Russia. That's why they risked their national existence to pursue weapons of mass destruction. The pandemonium created by a worldwide nuclear war matches the conditions they think will bring back the Mahdi.

Sunni extremists are dangerous, but not in the same way. Sunni terrorists are dangerous to malls, stadiums, even entire cities, while Shiite extremists threaten whole nations.

Both Sunnis and Shiites regard Israel as the enemy. But the two factions are also enemies of each other. Sunnis and Shiites have been fighting a holy war against each other since shortly after Mohammed died in AD 632.

Ezekiel 38 is the only place in the Bible where Persia is called an enemy to Israel. History bears this out. Until recent times, Persia was always a friend to Israel. Remember how the Babylonians stole Daniel and other Jews and took them captive? Then Persia defeated the Babylonians. Cyrus was the Persian king who allowed Israel to go back home to Jerusalem.

The Persian civilization became one of the most advanced in the history of the world. They were blessed immeasurably because they blessed the offspring of Abraham, Isaac, and Jacob (Genesis 12:3). But this chapter in Ezekiel warned that in the end times, Persia would become Israel's enemy. Today, Iran/Persia is an existential threat to Israel, making them mortal enemies. That's one more sign that we're living near the end of the age.

END TIME SURPRISE

Sometimes evangelical Christians see nothing but gloom and doom among Muslims. They see a quarter of the world's population as hopeless. They can't imagine Muslims coming to know Jesus, but they're forgetting the power of the gospel. Muslims are coming to Christ today in unprecedented numbers, and it's going to get better.

Isaiah 19 talks about Egypt in the last of the last days. "In that day five cities in the land of Egypt will speak the language of Canaan and swear by the Lord of hosts; one will be called the City of Destruction. In that day there will be an altar to the Lord in the midst of the land of Egypt, and a pillar to the Lord at its border. And it will be for a sign and for a witness to the Lord of hosts in the land of Egypt; for they will cry to the Lord because of the oppressors, and He will send them a Savior and a Mighty One, and He will deliver them" (Isaiah 19:18-20).

Notice the phrase "because of the oppressors." Right now that region is full of oppressors. ISIS is only the best known. As expected, with terrorists on all sides, people there live in fear. They live in an oppressive climate where one wrong move could mean the loss of one's tongue or head.

The oppressors' evil gives Egyptians and everyone else a look into the heart of Islam. That's one reason so many Muslims are turning from the darkness of Islam to the light of Christ.

Daniel says that in the last of the last days, Jordan will not fall to the Antichrist. Egypt will be beaten up by the Antichrist, but as a result, will turn to Jesus. Former Muslims in surprising numbers will refuse to bow the knee to Antichrist. They will turn instead to the Lord of the universe.

AMERICA

Where is America when the armies of Gog push into Israel from Russia, Iran, Turkey, and elsewhere? Look again at verse 13. "Sheba, Dedan, the merchants of Tarshish, and all their young lions will say to you, 'Have you come to take plunder? Have you gathered your army to take booty, to carry away silver and gold, to take away livestock and goods, to take great plunder?'" (Ezekiel 38:13).

The areas of Sheba and Dedan are in modern Saudi Arabia. Tarshish is Great Britain—so it's referring to "the merchants of Great Britain." "All their young lions will say to you, 'Have you come to take plunder? Have you gathered your army to take booty?'"

What are they doing? Protesting. Saudi Arabia is the home of Sunni Islam, so it protests when Shiite Iran makes this invasion with Russia. Great Britain, with its vast Sunni population, also protests. "All the young lions" of Great Britain could include the United States.

At best, America merely sits on the sidelines protesting Russia's move into Israel. That does not sound like a superpower. And yet, other important things will happen before Gog leads the invasion into Israel. It might not be as dire for America as it sounds.

EIGHT

A STOPPED CLOCK

Daniel 9 contains one of the great prophecies of the Bible. It contains specific numbers of years that correspond to specific dates in history. It prophesied key events centuries in advance of those events. And they happened to the day. It also gives us the foundation for understanding America's and Europe's future as the end of the age approaches.

In verse 24, the angel Gabriel said to Daniel, "Seventy weeks are determined for your people and for your holy city."

"Your people" means Israel and "your holy city" means Jerusalem. Theologians try to cut Israel out of the plan of God by misapplying this passage to the church. But the words are unequivocal. This message and the timetable it contains are for Daniel's people, and Daniel's people are the Jews. This is also about the fate of the holy city of Daniel's people—Jerusalem.

In Hebrew, the words translated "seventy weeks" literally mean "seventy sevens." Seventy times seven equals 490. So we're talking about 490 of some measuring unit of time. It can't be days or hours because neither of those would give enough time for this vast and far reaching prophecy to be fulfilled.

Weeks of years were a common concept to the Jews in those days. Leviticus 25:8 says, "And you shall count seven sabbaths of years for yourself." Earlier in the chapter, Daniel had been thinking and praying about a prophecy from Jeremiah that had to do with this concept. It seems obvious that Daniel would have seen the sevens as years. And, as we're about to see, history proves that they were indeed years.

Seventy weeks of years totals 490 years. The angel then divided the years into three sections—7 weeks (49 years), 62 weeks (434 years), and then one last week (7 years).

> "Know therefore and understand," Gabriel said, "that from the going forth of the command to restore and build Jerusalem until Messiah the Prince, there shall be seven weeks and sixty-two weeks; the street shall be built again, and the wall, even in troublesome times" (Daniel 9:25).

We know it took forty-nine years from the time the command went out to restore Jerusalem until they completed the job. The forty-nine years were indeed "troublesome times." We know that 434 years after that, Jesus presented Himself to Israel as Messiah. He entered Jerusalem sitting on a donkey as the prophets said He would. People waved palm branches and cried, "Hosanna to the Son of David! Blessed is He who comes in the name of the Lord!" (Matthew 21:9).

A PAUSE IN THE PROPHECY

Then the clock stopped ticking. The first two segments of the prophecy had been consecutive, but the third segment could not immediately follow the second. We know this because the prophecy tells us about two things that must happen between the end of the sixty-ninth week and before the beginning of the seventieth week. Daniel 9:26 says, "And after the sixty-two weeks Messiah shall be cut off, but not for Himself; And the people of the prince who is to come Shall destroy the city and the sanctuary."

The restoration of Jerusalem took seven weeks of years. Sixty-two weeks of years after that, Messiah would be "cut off." Both of those events happened to the day.

It says, "Messiah shall be cut off, but not for Himself." Jesus was crucified, not for Himself but for us. He died for our sins.

Messiah would be "cut off" "after" the sixty-ninth week. Jesus presented Himself to the nation of Israel as Messiah on the precise day of the fulfillment of the prophecy. A week "after" He presented Himself to the nation, He was crucified, "cut off."

Also after the sixty-ninth week, the prophecy said that Jerusalem would be destroyed. In AD 70, the Romans sacked Jerusalem and destroyed the Temple.

Those two prophecies were fulfilled after the sixty-ninth week. Could they have happened in the seventieth week? No. The seventieth week only lasts seven years, and Rome sacked Jerusalem forty years after the crucifixion of Jesus.

Also, the angel told Daniel exactly when the seventieth week begins. Daniel 9:27 says, "Then he shall confirm a covenant with many for one week." The antecedent of "he" is the prince who is to come whose people will sack Jerusalem and destroy the temple. The "prince who is to come" is Antichrist. So we know the seventieth week begins when the Antichrist signs his peace treaty with Israel.

Many prophecies contain elements that are not consecutive. Jesus illustrated this in Luke 4;

> He was handed the book of the prophet Isaiah. And when He had opened the book, He found the place where it was written: "The Spirit of

the Lord is upon Me, because He has anointed Me to preach the gospel to the poor; He has sent Me to heal the brokenhearted, to proclaim liberty to the captives and recovery of sight to the blind, to set at liberty those who are oppressed; to proclaim the acceptable year of the Lord."

Then He closed the book, and gave it back to the attendant and sat down. And the eyes of all who were in the synagogue were fixed on Him. And He began to say to them, "Today this Scripture is fulfilled in your hearing" (Luke 4:17-21).

The passage He read in Isaiah does not stop at "proclaim the acceptable year of the Lord." It only has a comma there. It goes on to talk about "the day of vengeance of our God" (Isaiah 61:2).

In His first coming, Jesus fulfilled everything in this messianic prophecy through "proclaim the acceptable year of the Lord." That's why Jesus said, "Today this Scripture is fulfilled in your hearing."

But "the day of vengeance of our God" is reserved for His Second Coming. The comma between those two phrases in Isaiah 61:2 has lasted two thousand years.

This is a regular feature of Bible prophecy. There is an old illustration of a man driving toward a distant mountain. Though far away, he sees certain features of the mountain. When he comes closer, he sees that he has been looking at two mountains—both of them real, but separated in space. Later, he finds himself in the valley between the two mountains. He didn't originally see the space between the mountains, but that does not make the mountains themselves any less real.

Even though the first two segments of the prophecy ran consecutively, the prophecy didn't say that all three sections would be contiguous to one another. It said only that there would be seventy weeks of years, and it specifically divided the 490 years into three parts—forty-nine years, 434 years, and seven years. The prophecy then goes on to give very specific information about the last seven years.

Verse 24 of Daniel 9 lists some of the things that will be accomplished during the 490 years. "to finish the transgression, to make an end of sins, to make reconciliation for iniquity, to bring in everlasting righteousness, to seal up vision and prophecy, and to anoint the Most Holy."

If all seventy weeks were in the past, all these things would have already happened to Israel. None of them have. This too shows that the seventieth week remains in the future. The clock on the 490 years will not start ticking again until Antichrist signs his peace treaty with Israel. Then, three-and-a-half years after the treaty signing ceremony, Antichrist will break the agreement.

THE SEVENTIETH WEEK

Daniel 9:27 says that Antichrist "shall confirm a covenant with many for one week; but in the middle of the week He shall bring an end to sacrifice and offering. And on the wing of abominations shall be one who makes desolate, even until the consummation, which is determined, is poured out on the desolate."

Jesus warned about the events of Daniel 9:27. He said, "When you see the 'abomination of desolation,' spoken of by Daniel the prophet, standing in the holy place" (whoever reads, let him understand), "then let those who are in Judea flee to the mountains. Let him who is on the housetop not go down to take anything out of his house. And let him who is in the field not go back to get his clothes" (Matthew 24:15-18).

This is a warning to the Jews. When you see this thing in the temple, run! Get out of town! The world is about to be shaken like never before, and Jerusalem will be the center of it all. The last three-and-a-half years of Daniel's seventieth week are known as the great tribulation. Jeremiah 30:7 calls it "the time of Jacob's trouble." The earth-shattering events described so vividly in Revelation all begin with the "'abomination of desolation.'"

So what will the abomination be? What horrible thing will the Antichrist do? Daniel makes it clear that this is more than just breaking a treaty. Something will happen in the Temple—inside the Holy of Holies. In 167 B.C., a Greek named Antiochus Epiphanies set up a pagan altar in the Temple to honor Zeus, and sacrificed a pig on the altar. This event became known as "the abomination of desolation."

This foreshadowed, but did not fulfill Daniel's prophecy. We know that the abomination was yet future because Jesus spoke of it as a future event. He said, "When you see the 'abomination of desolation,' spoken of by Daniel the prophet, standing in the holy place" (Matthew 24:15). Antiochus Epiphanes desecrated the temple in 167 B.C. long before Jesus said those words. So the ultimate fulfillment of the prophecy had not yet occurred.

ABOMINATION!

What specifically will the Antichrist do? Revelation 13:8 says, "All who dwell on the earth will worship him, whose names have not been written in the Book of Life of the Lamb slain from the foundation of the world." Verse 12 says the false prophet will compel people to worship the

Antichrist. Revelation 13:15 says that those who refuse to worship him will be executed.

Second Thessalonians 2:4 speaks of the time when the Antichrist "sits as God in the temple of God, showing himself that he is God."

The Antichrist—not just a mere human being, but a human being possessed by Satan—will stride into the Holy of Holies and present himself as God to be worshiped. It is an almost unfathomable abomination.

His action will "bring an end to sacrifice and offering" (Daniel 9:27). It will so desecrate the rebuilt temple that it can never again be used for those purposes. But that's okay because this is the beginning of the time when the nation of Israel will turn *en masse* to Jesus Christ. After this, they won't need daily or yearly sacrifices. They will receive full benefit of the once-and-for-all sacrifice of Christ on the cross (Hebrews 10:11-12).

Jesus was speaking to the Jews when He said, "O Jerusalem, Jerusalem, the one who kills the prophets and stones those who are sent to her! How often I wanted to gather your children together, as a hen gathers her chicks under her wings, but you were not willing! See! Your house is left to you desolate; for I say to you, you shall see Me no more till you say,

'Blessed is He who comes in the name of the Lord!'"
(Matthew 23:37-39).

Before they see Him return to the world at the end of
the tribulation, they will have turned to Him as their Lord
and Savior. They will rejoice when they see Him, saying,
"Blessed is He who comes in the name of the Lord!"

AMERICA AND EUROPE

Look back at Daniel 9:26. "And the people of the prince
who is to come shall destroy the city and the sanctuary.
The end of it shall be with a flood, and till the end of the
war desolations are determined."

Who destroyed Jerusalem and the sanctuary in AD 70?
The Romans! The "people of the prince who is to come"
are the people of the Roman empire. That means "the
prince who is to come"—the Antichrist—will be from the
region near the seat of the Roman Empire because he will
be from the people who destroyed Jerusalem in 70 AD.

Daniel 9:27—"Then he (the Antichrist) shall confirm a
covenant with many for one week." "Many" refers again
to Daniel's people, Israel. Antichrist will confirm a covenant with Israel for one week of years. Remember that
the 490 years were divided into three parts—that last part
lasting seven years.

In the middle of the seven years, the Antichrist will show his true nature. Verse 27 goes on, "But in the middle of the week he shall bring an end to sacrifice and offering. And on the wing of abominations shall be one who makes desolate, even until the consummation, which is determined, is poured out on the desolate."

So after three-and-a-half years, he's going to bring an end to sacrifice and offering. Right now there is no sacrifice because there is no Temple. This tells us that a new Temple will be built in Jerusalem sometime between now and the middle of Daniel's seventieth week.

Revelation 17 speaks of ten kings who will give their authority to the Antichrist. When the Bible says "kings," it usually means heads of state. In our century we might say Presidents or Prime Ministers. However, these will be "kings" without kingdoms.

> "The ten horns which you saw are ten kings who have received no kingdom as yet, but they receive authority for one hour as kings with the beast" (Revelation 17:12).

The world will be divided into ten regions, and ruled by this leader who rises out of Europe. Some Bible prophecy teachers have said (and I used to agree) that the ten kings came only out of Europe. But to see the real power of the ten kings, I think we should look at the power of the Antichrist after they transfer their authority to him.

RULE OF THE BEAST

Revelation 13:7-8 says, "Authority was given him (the Antichrist) over every tribe, tongue, and nation. All who dwell on the earth will worship him, whose names have not been written in the Book of Life of the Lamb slain from the foundation of the world."

So, he will rule the world but he will not obliterate the national structures already in place. For instance, there will still be a nation called France, but it will subordinate itself to the new supernational government run by the Antichrist.

The Antichrist will be the most acclaimed man ever, but only briefly. Rebellions will be in the wind not long after he comes to power.

The Antichrist's government will be based on the idea of global federalism. The U.S. federal government has certain jurisdictions, state governments have others, and local governments have others. The Antichrist will lead a federal government of the world, with nation-states intact. The Bible indicates that the existing nations will submit to the Antichrist's world economic system. Current events indicate there will also be global environmental controls. Some level of military control will also be in the hands of the world government. These areas of control match the great fears of our time—economic collapse, climate change, and war.

Since the Antichrist comes to lead a federal government of the world after receiving the power of the ten kings, I believe the ten kings will lead regions of the world, and not just areas of Europe. The regional governments may start as trade agreements.

Though global in nature, the Antichrist's government will favor the west. Leaders naturally favor their home territories. The rebellions against him also indicate the western flavor of his power. The rebellions will be centered in Russia, Asia, Africa, and the Middle East. Apparently in Europe and the Americas, he will remain something of a favorite son.

KINGS OF THE EAST

The last few years have seen stunning growth in China's financial, technical, industrial, and military power. To achieve these things, China borrowed heavily. The debt is creating tremendous upheaval in China's economy. Nevertheless, it remains the manufacturing colossus of the modern world. If economic desperation shifts more of its industrial power toward the military, it could take the world on one wild ride.

> "Then the sixth angel poured out his bowl on the great river Euphrates, and its water was dried up, so that the way of the kings from the east might be prepared" (Revelation 16:12).

Typically, people say "the kings of the east" means China. That could be true. China is massive and increasingly belligerent. Its goals are global. But the scriptural evidence may not be as strong as some think.

THE FORCE OF 200 MILLION

> "Then the sixth angel sounded: And I heard a voice from the four horns of the golden altar which is before God, saying to the sixth angel who had the trumpet, 'Release the four angels who are bound at the great river Euphrates.' So the four angels, who had been prepared for the hour and day and month and year, were released to kill a third of mankind. Now the number of the army of the horsemen was two hundred million; I heard the number of them. And thus I saw the horses in the vision: those who sat on them had breastplates of fiery red, hyacinth blue, and sulfur yellow; and the heads

of the horses were like the heads of lions; and out of their mouths came fire, smoke, and brimstone. By these three plagues a third of mankind was killed—by the fire and the smoke and the brimstone which came out of their mouths. For their power is in their mouth and in their tails; for their tails are like serpents, having heads; and with them they do harm" (Revelation 9:13-19).

Revelation speaks twice of the Euphrates River. The first reference is the one quoted immediately above from Revelation 9. In Revelation 16, there is another reference to the Euphrates. This time, "its water was dried up, so that the way of the kings from the east might be prepared" (Revelation 16:12).

In Revelation 9, there is no mention of the kings of the east. When it speaks of the army of 200 million, I believe it is referring to an army of demons. Reread the passage above to see what I mean. It describes a horde of 200 million demons that come out from underneath the Euphrates and wreak havoc on people all over the earth.

The river dries up later, close to the end of the seven-year tribulation. That's when the army of the East crosses the Euphrates on its way to Armageddon. The only connection with the 200 million is the Euphrates

River, but the scenarios are different. Despite the proficiency of the Chinese military, 200 million demons are a lot scarier than 200 million Chinese soldiers.

CHINA

A great deal of antagonism exists between East and West. In 2015, Chinese warships made a habit of approaching U.S. coastlines. Long-range Chinese bombers repeatedly flew to the edge of U.S. airspace. During Russia's military build-up in Syria, there were reports of a Chinese aircraft carrier aiding the Russians.

In recent years, Russia-China cooperation has hit an all-time high. When China's President Xi Jinping visited Moscow in 2013, Vladimir Putin said the two nations were forging a special relationship. The Russian-owned RT news service bragged about an "unprecedented show of military cooperation" during joint naval exercises in August of 2015.

As of this writing, the massive Chinese industrial machine is sputtering. Chinese debt stands at 282 percent of its gross domestic product. That makes even America's debt seem small. The U.S. debt is "only" a little more than 100 percent of GDP. China's debt comes from a gamble that it can take over much of the world's manufacturing. They've been building factories at an unprecedented rate, and now they've overbuilt.

In fact, excess manufacturing capacity is hurting the whole world's economy. Ambrose Evans-Pritchard, international business editor of the *The Daily Telegraph*, warns of "chronic overcapacity worldwide."

But the rest of the world didn't gamble as heavily as the Chinese. Their government tried lowering the value of their currency to make it easier for foreign markets to buy goods manufactured there, but it did no good. On several occasions in 2015 and 2016, their stock market fell so fast that the computers automatically halted trading. China may pull out of its economic tailspin, but some of the underlying factors don't look good.

And it's a fact of history that economic desperation often precedes military aggression.

OTHER KINGS OF THE EAST

People who study Bible prophecy almost automatically assume "kings of the east" means China. But don't forget that the scripture says "kings"—plural. It won't be a single nation.

North Korea might also be one of the "kings." In April of 2015, Admiral Bill Gortney, Commander of NATO, was asked at a press conference if North Korea had "developed the capability to miniaturize a nuclear warhead and put it on a ballistic missiles like the KN-08."

The Admiral answered, "Yes. Our assessment is that they have the ability to put it on—a nuclear weapon on a KN-08 and shoot it at the homeland."

North Korea is probably the poorest, most miserable country on the planet, yet it stands as a direct military threat to the richest, most powerful countries in the world. This kind of dichotomy will become more common in the future. Technology always trends downward in price and upward in availability. That applies to more than smart phones. It includes weapons. It allows an economically weak nation the kind of military strength needed to destabilize a region or the world.   .

North Korea is run by a small-minded, megalomaniacal thug. Its people are starving and oppressed. But it is a power on the world stage because it is a member of the nuclear club.

China and North Korea have had some spats recently, but their relationship is a long one. They are allies of the first order.

The "kings of the east" might also involve countries like Pakistan or even India. Both of those countries are nuclear powers.

In the Bible, "east" means east of the Euphrates River. That includes a lot of possibilities for the "kings of the east."

NINE

AMERICA AND ISRAEL

Through Moses, God made a covenant with the nation of Israel. Unlike the covenant He made with Abraham, this one was conditional. They had to keep the law. God promised to keep His end of the bargain if they kept theirs. In Deuteronomy 28, God tells the people some of the amazing ways He will bless them if they obey His law.

Then, starting in verse 15, he tells them what will happen if they do not obey. "But it shall come to pass, if you do not obey the voice of the LORD your God, to observe carefully all His commandments and His statutes which I command you today, that all these curses will come upon you and overtake you" (Deuteronomy 28:15).

In Deuteronomy 28:64, He's still telling them the bad things that will happen if they break their side of the covenant. "The LORD will scatter you among all peoples, from one end of the earth to the other."

On many occasions, God promised to scatter the Jews. He also promised to bring them back to the land. We might expect Him to bring them back to the land after they repent of the sins that caused them to be scattered. Yet He promised to do just the opposite.

God gave a summary of His plan for Israel to the prophet Ezekiel.

> "I poured out My fury on them for the blood they had shed on the land, and for their idols with which they had defiled it. So I scattered them among the nations, and they were dispersed throughout the countries; I judged them according to their ways and their deeds. When they came to the nations, wherever they went, they profaned My holy name—when they said of them, 'These are the people of the LORD, and yet they have gone out of His land.' But I had concern for My holy name, which the house of Israel had profaned among the nations wherever they went.
>
> "Therefore say to the house of Israel, 'Thus says the Lord GOD: "I do not do this for your sake, O house of Israel, but for My holy name's sake, which you have profaned among the nations wherever you went. And I will sanctify

My great name, which has been profaned
among the nations, which you have profaned
in their midst; and the nations shall know that
I am the LORD,' says the Lord GOD, 'when I
am hallowed in you before their eyes. For I will
take you from among the nations, gather you
out of all countries, and bring you into your
own land. Then I will sprinkle clean water on
you, and you shall be clean; I will cleanse you
from all your filthiness and from all your idols.
I will give you a new heart and put a new spirit
within you; I will take the heart of stone out
of your flesh and give you a heart of flesh'"'"
(Ezekiel 36:18-26).

"I do not do this for your sake, O house of Israel," the
Lord God said, "but for My holy name's sake, which you
have profaned among the nations wherever you went....
I will take you from among the nations, gather you out of
all countries, and bring you into your own land."

Then, after all that, He promised to give them "a new
heart."

God keeps His word. When He said "for My holy name's
sake," He was saying He will keep His name good. He will
keep His word. He signed His name on the check and you
can bank on it! In Genesis 12:1–3, God made promises

to Abraham that did not depend on any future action by Abraham or his descendants.

THE COVENANT WITH ABRAHAM

He reiterated the covenant in Genesis 15. It is there that God makes crystal clear that the covenant's fulfillment depends only on Him, and not on Abraham or his descendants. Abraham wanted something to help him be more sure, and God graciously gave it to him.

The Lord told Abraham to prepare for a ceremony that was for two men of that time and region when entering into a formal covenant together. God told Abraham to find a heifer, a goat, a ram, a turtledove, and a young pigeon. Abraham cut the three larger animals in half, and laid the halves opposite one another.

Normally in this ceremony, the two parties making a covenant would walk between the halved animals. It meant, "May this happen to me if I do not fulfill my part of this covenant."

Abraham prepared for the ceremony, then waited through the heat of the day. He kept watch over the ceremonial animals. Birds would swoop in and try to eat them, but Abraham shooed them away. Verse 12 says, "Now when the sun was going down, a deep sleep fell upon Abram; and behold, horror and great darkness fell upon him."

During this time, God spoke to Abraham about several important things including his descendants and the land. After that, Abraham saw something astounding.

> "And it came to pass, when the sun went down and it was dark, that behold, there appeared a smoking oven and a burning torch that passed between those pieces. On the same day the LORD made a covenant with Abram, saying: "To your descendants I have given this land, from the river of Egypt to the great river, the River Euphrates" (Genesis 15:17-18).

Abraham expected the two of them to pass between the animals together, signifying that both would be responsible for the covenant's fulfillment. But God passed between the animals alone. Both the smoking oven and burning torch signified God's presence. He performed the ceremony with Himself. He alone would be responsible for the fulfillment of the covenant.

That's why He said through Ezekiel, "I do not do this for your sake, O house of Israel, but for My holy name's sake."

His good name depends on His fidelity to His promises.

RETURN TO THE LAND

For the last century and a half, He has been bringing Jews back to the land because He promised that land to Abraham, Isaac, Jacob, and their descendants. He made a covenant with their fathers, starting with Abraham. Through Moses, He said that if they disobeyed they would be scattered, and they were. It is for His "holy name's sake" that He is bringing them back as He said He would.

God's protection of the Jews as a distinct people through-out the centuries while they lived scattered among nations, is an epic miracle. Bringing them back and renewing their ownership of the land is even more astounding. It is a parting of the Red Sea kind of miracle. God made a promise to Abraham regarding the land. We see it coming true before our eyes.

He also made this promise. "I will bless those who bless you, and I will curse him who curses you" (Genesis 12:3). We see that happening, too.

GOD BLESSES AMERICA

No nation in the world has been as generous to the Jewish people as the United States of America—nor has any nation ever been so blessed. It's not a coincidence.

In 1948, Harry Truman's foreign policy team was dead set against the United States recognizing the new State of Israel. His Secretary of State, George Marshall, was so adamant that he told the President, "If you decide to recognize Israel, I will vote against you in the next election."

Truman took the risk that he would lose the vote of his leading cabinet member, the man he placed in charge of foreign policy, and chose to recognize Israel. Eleven minutes after Israel declared its independence, the United States government gave it official recognition, the first nation in the world to do so. America went on to become Israel's primary supporter and friend among the nations of the world.

Later, Truman would say, "I had faith in Israel before it was established, I have faith in it now."

The years before that decision, America had been through two world wars and the great depression. The years that followed saw a level of economic growth and near-universal prosperity unprecedented in the history of nations.

More recently, America has done some deadly things. First, it has systematically and officially turned away from God on an institutional level. As a result, moral standards fell like a rock. Not coincidentally, America turned away from Israel during the same time.

Zechariah 12 speaks of the last days. Verse 3 says, "And it shall happen in that day that I will make Jerusalem a very heavy stone for all peoples; all who would heave it away will surely be cut in pieces, though all nations of the earth are gathered against it."

Daniel 11 gives the same idea. Then in Zechariah 12:9 God said, "It shall be in that day that I will seek to destroy all the nations that come against Jerusalem."

That is another fulfillment of God's promise to Abraham in Genesis 12. "I will bless those who bless you, and I will curse him who curses you."

Through Zechariah, God said that one day all the world will turn against Jerusalem (Zechariah 12:3). America is already headed in that direction. When the U.S. pushes Israel to divide Jerusalem, it joins the side of the Antichrist. Recent U.S. Presidents of both parties have used our nation's special relationship with Israel to pressure Israeli leaders to accommodate unreasonable Palestinian demands, and place the people of both sides in ever greater danger.

THE IRAN NUCLEAR DEAL

The Obama Administration practically blackmailed Israel not to take out Iran's nuclear program. Instead, it pushed through a nuclear weapons agreement with Iran that seems certain to give Israel's nearby enemy such weapons within ten years. In an act reminiscent of the European colonialism of centuries past, those negotiating with Iran did not include any of the countries most immediately affected—Iran's Mid-East neighbors, especially Israel.

First Thessalonians 5:2-3 says, "For you yourselves know perfectly that the day of the Lord so comes as a thief in the night. For when they say, 'Peace and safety!' then sudden destruction comes upon them, as labor pains upon a pregnant woman. And they shall not escape."

After the Iran deal, Joel Rosenberg wrote, "U.S. and world leaders keep saying the Iran deal will bring 'peace and safety.' They repeat it like a mantra."

Rosenberg gave several examples, starting with the opening paragraph of the Iran deal itself.

> • "This historic Joint Comprehensive Plan of Action (JCPOA)…will ensure that Iran's nuclear programme will be exclusively peaceful….This JCPOA will positively contribute to regional and international peace and security."

> • UN Secretary General Ban Ki-Moon said the Iran deal "could serve as a vital contribution

to peace and stability both in the region and beyond."

• President Obama called it a "victory for diplomacy...the safety and security of the world."

• Representative Patrick Murphy used wording that is cringe-worthy to anyone familiar with the history of World War II. He spoke of "peace in our time."

• Representative Keith Ellison said, "We can choose peace over war. The world is safer."

• Representative Derek Kilmer said, "The proposed agreement with Iran...puts us on a path toward a safer and more peaceful world."

Where are we on God's prophetic calendar? Claims of "peace and safety" give us another clue.

AMERICA IN BIBLE PROPHECY

Does the Bible ever speak specifically about the United States of America? Some say that America is Mystery Babylon from Revelation 17 and 18. That would put the U.S. at the heart of Bible prophecy, but the evidence for this seems thin.

Others point to various prophetic passages that reference the eagle. The United States chose the bald eagle as its official bird back in 1782, but the eagle is a fairly popular national symbol. Poland, Germany, and Romania all claim it today. Several nations from antiquity also used the eagle as their symbol, including Rome.

Some say America is included with the far off coast lands or islands mentioned in Ezekiel 39:6 when the Gog and Magog war starts. The evidence here is also unconvincing.

At best, America may be one of the nations protesting the last days war when Russia and Persia invade Israel in Ezekiel 38. While that's a distinct possibility, it doesn't say much for America's future as a superpower, or even as a particularly influential member of the family of nations.

That bothers a lot of people. It bothers me, too. Even now, the United States remains the greatest nation in the world. In some ways, it's the greatest nation in the history of the world. It's upsetting to hear someone say that America will not be a significant player during the last days. The Bible identifies the significant players in the last days—Russia, Iran, many of the Islamic countries, Asia, Europe, and Israel.

What can we expect in America's future? The nation seems headed down a dark, slippery path away from God's blessing. The world does not revolve around the United States of America. And, for whatever reason, God seems to have determined not to make America the superpower of the last days, or even one of the main players.

We know God will judge America. Yes, it is a better, more moral place than many others around the world, but we must remember a principle articulated by Jesus in Luke 12:48, "For everyone to whom much is given, from him much will be required."

America essentially disappears in Bible prophecy. It may simply collapse. This could happen in any number of ways. It could be a victim of its own moral degradation. It's as if America has AIDS, a disease that destroys its victim's immune system. With a compromised immune system, the AIDS patient can no longer fight off disease. America's immune system is its morality, and that morality grows weaker by the day.

We've robbed ourselves of the strength to fight off any kind of long term or severe threat. Could today's America fight a world war, or survive an economic collapse as severe as the Great Depression? In this weakened state, America is vulnerable to terrorism, conventional or nuclear war, an internal uprising, or any number of debilitating possibilities.

AMERICA'S HOPE

Near the beginning of the book, I laid out another possibility. Perhaps we will have another Great Awakening in America that will bring vast portions of the population to Christ. That would make the rapture a devastating event for the U.S. economy and defense. So many Christians could be caught up into heaven that it leaves their earth-bound countrymen scrambling to get by.

One way or another, America will not be in a position of preeminence by the time the Antichrist rises to power. But if Americans will seek God, turn away from wickedness and to Him, things can improve dramatically right up to the time of the rapture. Jesus warned us of persecution in the last days. The answer, though, is not fear and it's certainly not to begin espousing unbiblical doctrine. Paradoxically, it may be possible to decrease persecution by living all out for God. Compromise of the gospel will only make things worse.

Although the future may hold difficulties for Christ's disciples, God has made a way of escape from the worst tribulation. Jesus said, "Watch therefore, and pray always that you may be counted worthy to escape all these things that will come to pass, and to stand before the Son of Man" (Luke 21:36).

"To escape all these things" refers to the rapture. You don't want to be around for the days of great tribulation Jesus warned of in Matthew 24:21. "There will be great tribulation, such as has not been since the beginning of the world until this time, no, nor ever shall be."

The Bible's silence on America indicates that by the time of the Ezekiel 38 invasion of Israel, America no longer stands as a world power. We can hope that its diminished state will be a result of the number of people taken from the U.S. at the rapture of the church.

THE RAPTURE

First Thessalonians 4:13-18 gives a vivid description of the rapture. Notice the use of the word "asleep" to speak of the redeemed dead. Paul here is following the lead of Jesus in calling them "asleep". It's not a reference to what some call "soul sleep." Rather, it is a statement of faith regarding the resurrection of the dead in Christ.

> "But I do not want you to be ignorant, brethren, concerning those who have fallen asleep, lest you sorrow as others who have no hope. For if we believe that Jesus died and rose again, even so God will bring with Him those who sleep in Jesus. For this we say to you by the word of the Lord, that we who are alive and remain until

the coming of the Lord will by no means pre-
cede those who are asleep. For the Lord Himself
will descend from heaven with a shout, with the
voice of an archangel, and with the trumpet of
God. And the dead in Christ will rise first. Then
we who are alive and remain shall be caught up
together with them in the clouds to meet the
Lord in the air. And thus we shall always be
with the Lord. Therefore comfort one another
with these words" (1 Thessalonians 4:13-18).

People have said to me, "You teach on the rapture
because you just want to escape all that stuff. You're an
escapist."

Exactly! That's what Jesus said to do. "Watch therefore,
and pray always that you may be counted worthy to escape
all these things." How am I worthy? My worthiness is in
the Lord Jesus Christ!

Acts 2:17 says, "And it shall come to pass in the last days,
says God, that I will pour out of My Spirit on all flesh."

As we come to the last of the last days, I see that happening and expect that to increase. I pray that a great
awakening will come upon America, and the whole world.

Whether by rapture, continued moral collapse, or a
severe and sudden moral collapse that follows the rapture,

America will be severely weakened. A new world order is coming, and we can see the groundwork for it being laid even now.

A FINAL WORD

The future depicted in this book can be frightening, comforting, or both. It's comforting because it proves that in the Bible we hear from God. Bible prophecy is God's signature on His work. Only He could have predicted 2,000 years ago the alignment of nations today.

If He can do that, you can also trust the other things He says. He says He will care for His people, and He will. But maybe you're not one of those people. Maybe you've never received the forgiveness Jesus died to give you. Anyone who receives His sacrifice on the cross for their sin is forgiven. Anybody who does not receive that sacrifice is not forgiven.

You have two options. You can know Christ, receive forgiveness, and go to heaven. You can reject Him, and go to hell—be separated from Him, and from all that is good and meaningful for eternity. He wants you to recognize you're a sinner and acknowledge that to Him. He wants you to ask Him for forgiveness, and to repent of your sins. Repent means to turn from those sins.

He wants you to receive His grace. Grace is the unmerited favor of God. You don't earn it. It's a gift. All you have to do is receive it. Yes, it will change you. You will not be the person you were, but the change in the way you live does not save you. Change is the by-product—not the cause—of His grace. Grace alone saves.

On the next page is a suggested prayer. You don't have to use these words. Also, just reciting some words will do you no good. But if you pray it and mean it, you will receive His grace, and be born anew.

> Dear Lord Jesus, I recognize that I am a sinner. And I ask You to forgive me. I repent of my sins, and I surrender to You. Thank You for forgiving me. In Jesus' name I pray. Amen.